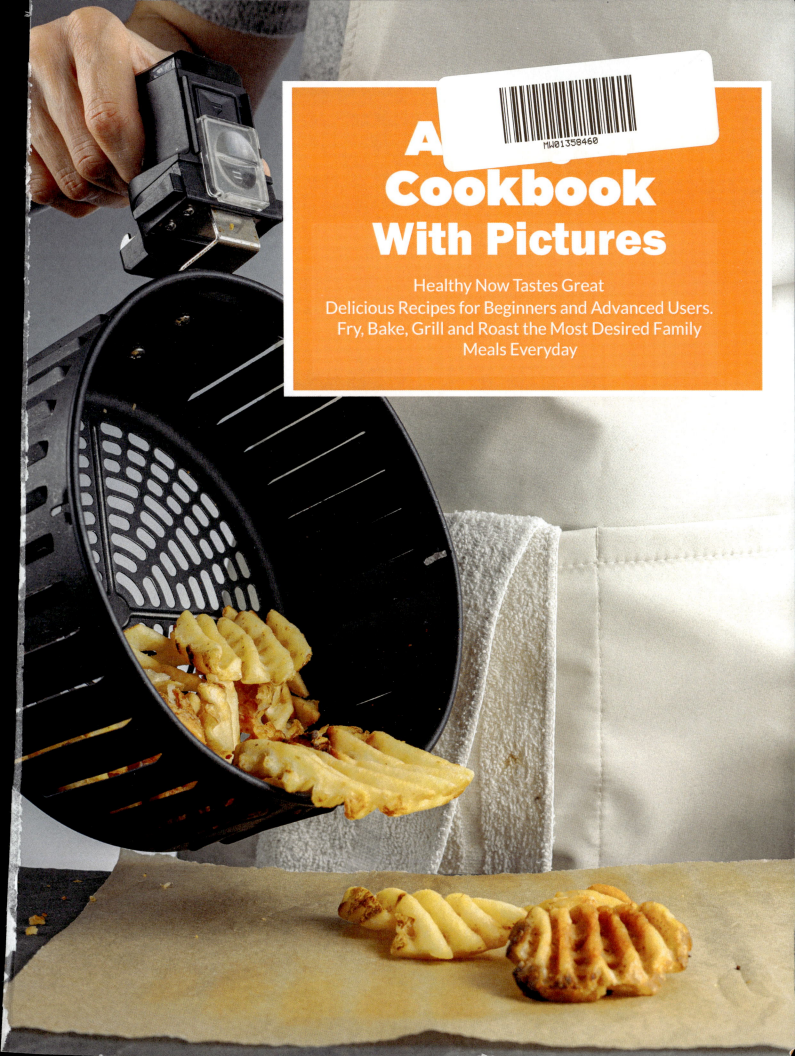

Air Fryer Cookbook With Pictures

Healthy Now Tastes Great
Delicious Recipes for Beginners and Advanced Users.
Fry, Bake, Grill and Roast the Most Desired Family Meals Everyday

Copyright - 2021 - All rights reserved.

The content contained within this book may not be reproduced, duplicated or transmitted without direct written permission from the author or the publisher.Under no circumstances will any blame or legal responsibility be held against the publisher, or author, for any damages, reparation, or monetary loss due to the information contained within this book. Either directly or indirectly.

Legal Notice

This book is copyright protected. This book is only for personal use. You cannot amend, distribute, sell, use, quote or paraphrase any part, or the content within this book, without the consent of the author or publisher.

Disclaimer Notice

Please note the information contained within this document is for educational and entertainment purposes only. All effort has been executed to present accurate, up to date, and reliable, complete information. No warranties of any kind are declared or implied. Readers acknowledge that the author is not engaging in the rendering of legal, financial, medical or professional advice. The content within this book has been derived from various sources. Please consult a licensed professional before attempting any techniques outlined in this book. By reading this document, the reader agrees that under no circumstances is the author responsible for any losses, direct or indirect, which are incurred as a result of the use of information contained within this document, including, but not limited to, - errors, omissions, or inaccuracies.

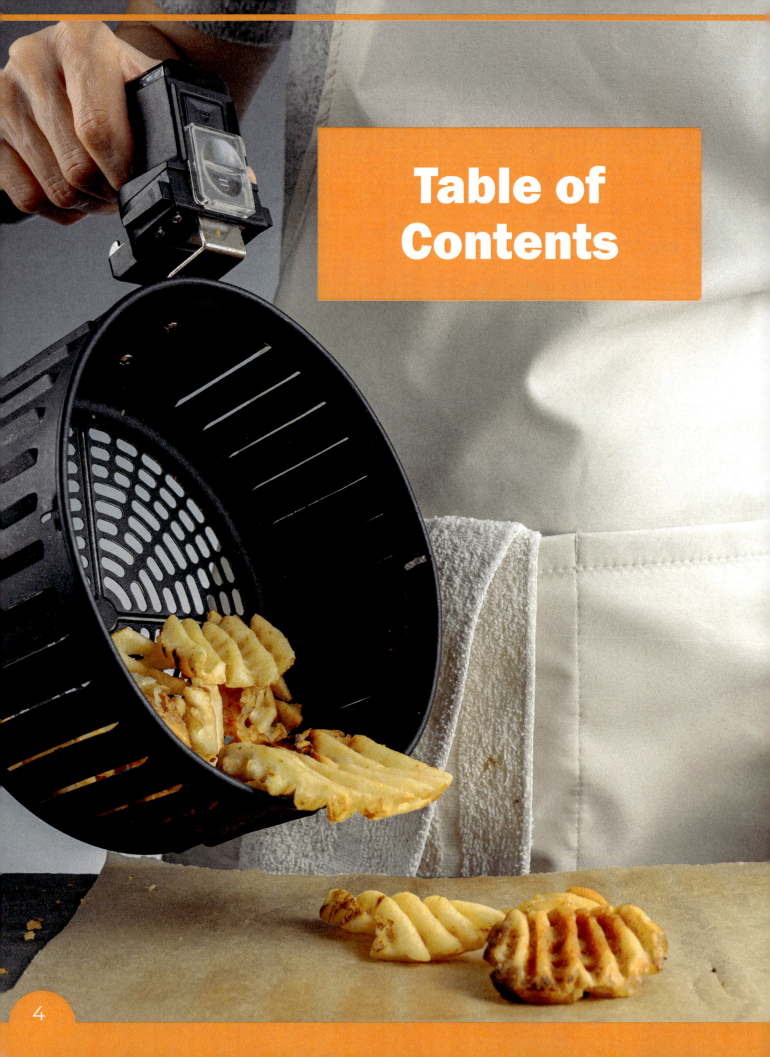

Table of Contents

INTRODUCTION TO AIR FRYER	6
CHAPTER 1 **BASICS OF AIR FRYER**	8
CHAPTER 2 **BREAKFAST RECIPES**	12
CHAPTER 3 **VEGETABLE RECIPES**	17
CHAPTER 4 **FISH AND SEAFOOD RECIPES**	23
CHAPTER 5 **RED MEAT RECIPES**	29
CHAPTER 6 **POULTRY RECIPES**	36
CHAPTER 7 **ROTISSERIE RECIPES**	44
CHAPTER 8 **APPETIZERS AND SNACKS RECIPES**	49
CHAPTER 9 **DELICIOUS DESSERT RECIPES**	55
CHAPTER 10 **HOLIDAY SPECIAL RECIPES**	62
CHAPTER 11 **GLUTEN-FREE RECIPES**	67
CHAPTER 12 **WRAPS AND SANDWICHES RECIPES**	73
CHAPTER 13 **15-MINUTES AIR FRYER RECIPES**	77
CONCLUSION	83
AIR FRYER COOKING CHART	85

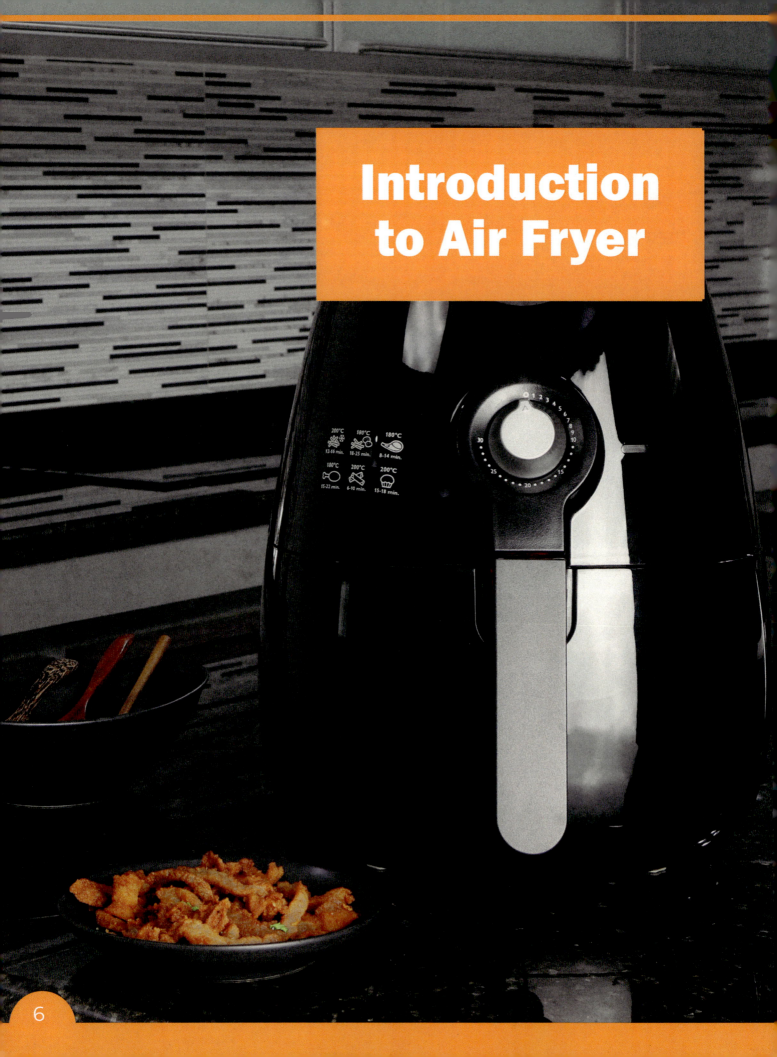

Introduction to Air Fryer

Air fryer recipes are sweeping the nation.
And There's no question that air fryers are hugely popular: but it's so much more than a gimmicky kitchen tool.

An air fryer is essentially a countertop convection oven that allows deep frying with the least oil (can heat up in minutes and blasts more direct air than a regular convection oven could ever do).

Air-fried food is as tasty as it's advertised to be and the air fryer cooks the food so quite evenly, so chicken, fish and other proteins come out juicy on the inside while crisp out.

Yes, eliminating the need for oil makes eating healthier a whole lot easier.

There are all kinds of things you can air-fry: from mains and sides to desserts and snacks.

I have prepared a wide variety of different recipes with colorful pictures for you. I have tried every single one of these recipes and have been tried and tested by others.

Making authentic fried food at home is virtually impossible without an air fryer

No matter if you're looking for an easy entree for tonight, a gluten-free recipe or something to cure that sweet tooth: you'll find the best recipe for you below.

Basics of Air Fryer

How it Works

Air fryers cook food that would otherwise be submerged in oil by circulating hot air. The frying chamber of an air fryer radiates heat from a heating element near the food, and a fan circulates hot air. Depending on the model, temperatures can reach 482°F.

Compared to non-convection ovens, cooking times in the air fryer can be lowered by up to 20%. The air fryer works by coating the desired food in a thin layer of oil, applying heat, and initiating the reaction with circulating air heated to 392°F.

As a result, the equipment can brown meals such as potato chips, poultry, fish, steak, cheeseburgers, French fries, or pastries with 70% to 80% less oil than a standard deep fryer.

Setting Panel

Temperature and timer adjustments are available on most air fryers, allowing for more exact cooking. Typically, food is cooked in a basket on a drip tray. The basket must be agitated regularly, either manually or with the help of an integrated food agitator. Air fryers are typically smaller and produce less heat. Because the larger amount of oil used in traditional frying permeates the foods (or the coating batter, if used) and adds its flavor, the taste and consistency of dishes prepared using traditional fried methods and air fried techniques are not identical.

Unboxing and Setup

While we all know how to unbox anything, let alone be an air fryer, but an important thing to check while unboxing the Air Fryer is to check whether you have all items mentioned below:

- Basket Release Button
- Crumb Basket
- Timer Control Knob
- Power on Indicator
- Air Inlet
- Air Outlet – you can find this at the backside of the air fryer
- Crumb Basket Handle
- Frying Basket
- Temperature Control Slider
- Heating Indicator
- Handle

Benefits of Air Fryer Oven

When you bite into a dish of fried chicken or French fries, you get the same taste of crisp crunch and moist, chewy hit right away. However, the delectable taste of fried dishes comes with a price. According to research, the oils used to cook them are linked to health issues such as heart disease, type 2 diabetes, and cancer. Air fryers are kitchen machines that promise the flavor, texture, and golden-brown color of oil-fried foods without the fat and calories.

Better Cooking

Air frying is healthier than frying in oil. It reduces calories by 70% to 80% and contains a lot less fat. This cooking method may help reduce some of the other negative consequences of oil frying. According to one study, air frying reduces the level of acrylamide in fried potatoes by 90%.

Air fryers can help you lose weight

Fried food consumption is directly linked to an increased risk of obesity. This is due to the high fat and calorie content of deep-fried dishes. Weight loss can be aided by switching from deep-fried to air-fried dishes and eliminating the regular intake of unhealthy oils.

Deep fryers aren't always as safe as air fryers

Deep-frying foods necessitates the use of a big container filled with hot oil. This might be dangerous. While air fryers do get hot, there is no danger of spilling, splashing, or touching boiling oil by accident.

Versatility

This is perhaps the most favorite aspect of an air fryer. It allows you to do a lot many things which might not be possible using the conventional oven. However, you can use it for baking, roast, broil, grill, and fry. Do you want to have chicken and snow peas for dinner? With one of them, it's simple to make. You can use them for cooking both frozen and fresh dishes, as well as to reheat leftovers. Meats, fish, casseroles, sandwiches, and various vegetables have all been prepared in mine. A grill, rotisserie rack, or preeminent cooking stands are included in some fryers. Because the baskets can be divided, you can prepare multiple foods. Amazingly, a single device can cook so many different foods in so many different ways.

Ease of use

Most fryers are simple to operate; simply set the temperature and cooking time, add the food, and then shake the fryer a few times during cooking. There's no need to fuss or stir like you would on a stovetop and the unit doesn't lose much heat when it's opened, so if you want to peek while cooking, go ahead! You won't be slowing things down as you would in an oven if you do this.

Energy efficiency

These fryers are more efficient than using an oven and will not overheat your home. I've been using mine throughout a heat wave, and I enjoy that it keeps my kitchen from being too hot. You will be impressed with how effective these units are if you attempt to keep your house cool during the summer or are concerned about your electric bill.

Cooking and Usage Tips

So, how can something be nutritious if it's fried? Easy! These gadgets can be operated without using any oil or with just a spray of oil if you like. You can prepare frozen fries, chicken wings, onion rings, and more without adding extra oil and still producing extremely crispy results.
I was blown away that my frozen fries were excellent after only 15 minutes in the oven, even though they typically require up to 45 minutes in the oven. You'll undoubtedly adore this time-saver if you need to cook snacks or meals quickly

Clean and Clear

Clean-up is one aspect of cooking that most of us dislike. You only need to clean an air fryer's basket and pan, and many are dishwasher safe. Food does not adhere to non-stick coated sections of the pan and instead slips right off onto your plate. It only takes a few minutes to clean up after each use. This encourages me to cook more at home because I don't have to worry about cleaning up!

What if you have a large family or many dinner guests? You can choose to use Iconites Air Fryer Oven

The Iconites 10-In-1 Air Fryer Oven is the perfect go-to if you're searching for a diverse approach to cook low-fat meals with minimal cleanup. With a capacity of 20 quarts, you'll be able to prepare a huge number of excellent dinners for your family and friends while still having leftovers. The Iconites 10-In-1 Air Fryer Oven cooks with very little oil. It works by blowing hot air around your food from within; the Heated air penetrates the ingredients and cooks the food well. You'll serve delectable dishes that will have your guests begging for more. This 10-in-1 gadget allows you to cook in a variety of ways while saving room in your kitchen. It may be used as a pizza grill, rotisserie, oven and dehydrator, and an air fryer. It may be used to make crispy wings, bake a flatbread, and dehydrate apple slices, among other things. It can withstand temperatures ranging from 180 °F to 40 °F. This model also includes a variety of handy accessories to aid in the preparation of your meals. When you want to prepare an entire chicken, a skewer rotisserie comes in useful. The dehydration racks make it simple to arrange the components for maximum exposure. A roasting basket, fetch rack, oven mitts, a fry net basket, and chicken fork are included with this air fryer. You simply press the pre-set selections on the LED digital touch screen to utilize the Iconites 10-In-1 Air Fryer Oven. The air fryer takes care of the rest once you choose the cooking option and add the ingredients.

Furthermore, many of the removable elements are dishwasher safe once the meal is done. Cleanup is quick and easy, so you can get back to enjoying the company of your family and friends. This selection is ideal if you're searching for a versatile cooking tool that can handle everything from roasting to air frying.

Accessories and Features of Iconites Air Fryer Oven

Following are the features of Iconites air fryer oven:

- For large families, entertaining, and leftovers, a 20-quart size is ideal.
- Air fryer, pizza grill, dehydrator, and oven toaster are the cooking options.
- The temperature ranges between 180 and 400°F.
- 1800 watts of electricity for evenly cooked food
- Cooking modes are available on the LED digital touch screen.
- Rotisserie skewer, oven mitts, drip tray, dehydrating racks, fry net basket, chicken fork, and roasting basket are among the 13 accessories.

Breakfast Recipes

1. Sausage and Egg Breakfast Burrito

25 min   Easy   6

Nutrition Facts
Per Serving: 638 calories; protein 25.6g; carbohydrates 44.9g; fat 39.1g; cholesterol 244.3mg; sodium 1180.9mg.

Ingredients:
- 6 eggs
- 3 tbsp. milk
- 1 lb. Odom's sausage
- ⅛ tsp. black pepper
- ¼ tsp. salt
- ½ cup chopped onion
- 1 can of diced tomatoes
- 6 tortillas
- 1 cup cheddar cheese (shredded)

Directions:
1. Preheat air fryer to 390°F.
2. Take a medium-sized bowl and whisk salt, pepper, egg and milk together.
3. Cook the sausages in the oiled air fryer for 5-10 minutes until they are brown, add tomatoes and onion, and cook for more than 2 minutes till the onions are tender. Take the mixture in a bowl and keep it aside.
4. Now cook the egg mixture till it is almost set.
5. Spoon the sausage mixture and press from the center. Top it with the scrambled eggs evenly.
6. Roll up the tortilla and cut.
7. Serve and enjoy.

2. Air Fryer Wontons

30 min   Medium   50

Nutrition Facts
Per Serving: 74 calories; protein 4.6g; carbohydrates 5.5g; fat 3.6g; cholesterol 14mg; sodium 113.6mg.

Ingredients:
- 1 lb. boneless chicken
- 1 tbsp. grated ginger
- 2 minced garlic cloves
- 2 tbsp. chopped scallions
- 1 tbsp. soy sauce
- 2 tbsp. chili sauce
- 2 cups chopped cabbage
- Olive oil for brushing

Directions:
1. Prepare the wonton wrappers according to the given instructions.
2. Mix all the ingredients in a bowl.
3. Take one wonton wrapper in hand and spoon the mixture over it.
4. Fold the wrapper and seal it.
5. Repeat the process.
6. Place in the air fryer and apply some cooking spray.
7. Cook to 370° F for 5-6 minutes/until they are golden brown and crispy.
8. Serve with the sauce.
9. Enjoy it.

3. Sauerkraut Fritter

240 min   Difficult   12

Nutrition Facts
Per Serving: 223 calories; protein 7.6g; carbohydrates 26.4g; fat 9.4g; cholesterol 24.2mg; sodium 412.2mg.

Ingredients:
For fritter:
- 16 oz. sauerkraut
- 1 sausage
- 6 oz. bacon (thick cut)
- 2 tbsp. mustard grain
- 3 oz. grated cheese
- 3 beaten eggs
- 1 cup panko crumbs

For breading:
- 1 ½ cup flour
- 1 tsp. salt and pepper
- 2 beaten eggs
- 1 ½ cup crumbs

Directions:
1. Drain the sauerkraut.
2. Cut the bacon and sausage.
3. Add the chopped bacon and sausage to the pan and drizzle with oil.
4. Cook till they become crispy and light brown.
5. Turn off the stove.
6. Add the drained sauerkraut.
7. Add the beaten eggs and mix well.
8. Cover the mixture and place it in the refrigerator for at least 3 hours.
9. Take the mixture out of the refrigerator and make small balls of it.
10. Mix all-purpose flour, pepper and salt in 1 bowl.
11. Take the beaten eggs into 2nd bowl.
12. Take crumbs in a 3rd bowl.
13. Roll the balls first in the flour mixture, dip in the beaten eggs, and coat with the crumbs.
14. Arrange the balls in the air fryer oven tray and apply some cooking spray.
15. Cook to 400°F for 5-10 minutes until they are golden brown and crispy.
16. Serve with the sauce.
17. Enjoy.

4. Homemade Cherry Breakfast Tarts

25 min   Easy   8

Nutrition Facts
Per Serving: 143 calories; protein 2.1g; carbohydrates 14.6g; fat 8.6g; cholesterol 34.3mg; sodium 95.3mg.

Ingredients:
- 4 sheets of puff pastry
- 1 beaten egg
- 2 tbsp. water
- 10 oz. cherry pie (canned)
- olive oil

Directions:
1. Take the sheets on a flat surface.
2. Cut the sheets into 4 squares, making a total of 8 squares.
3. Beat the egg in a bowl with water to make an egg wash.
4. Take a cooking brush and apply egg wash on each square.
5. Put ½ tbsp. cherry pie on the sheet.
6. Fold the sheet in a triangular shape.
7. Spritz the basket of the air fryer with some oil.
8. Cook the cherry pastries to 370° F for 8-10 minutes.
9. Let them cool.
10. Serve and enjoy.

5. Sausage and Cream Cheese Biscuits

45 min — Medium — 10

Nutrition Facts
Per Serving: 84 calories; protein 1.4g; carbohydrates 3.5g; fat 7.3g; cholesterol 16.4mg; sodium 166.3mg.

Ingredients:
- 1 tbsp. vegetable oil
- 2 beaten eggs
- ⅛ tsp. salt and pepper
- ¼ lb. bulk sausage
- 1 can of flaky biscuits
- 2 oz. cheddar cheese
- 1 tbsp. water
- 1 egg

Directions:
1. Cut the parchment paper into a round shape and spray it with the cooking spray.
2. Crumble the sausages in a pan for 3-5 minutes and transfer them to a bowl. Keep it aside.
3. Now add salt, eggs, and pepper to the pan and cook till the eggs are cooked.
4. Now add the egg mixture into the sausages.
5. Take the dough. Cut in the round shape. Spoon the egg sausage mixture over it and place one piece of cheese over it. Fold the biscuits and brush with egg wash.
6. Place the parchment paper in the air fryer oven tray and put the biscuits over it.
7. Cook the biscuits to 325° F for 8 minutes until the biscuits are crispy brown.
8. Serve and enjoy.

6. Fried Chicken and Waffles

50 min — Medium — 2

Nutrition Facts
Per Serving: 1783 calories; protein 72.9g; carbohydrates 127.1g; fat 109.9g; cholesterol 396.8mg; sodium 5234.2mg.

Ingredients:
- Fried buttermilk honey chicken
- 1 lb. boneless chicken
- 1 cup all-purpose flour
- 3 tsp. divided paprika
- 1 tbsp. corn starch
- 1 tsp. onion powder
- ½ tsp. salt and pepper
- 1 large egg
- 1 tsp. baking powder
- ½ cup buttermilk
- 1 tsp. baking soda
- 2 tbsp. honey
- Cooking spray

For waffles:
- 1 cup cornmeal
- 2 tsp. baking powder
- 1 cup all-purpose flour
- 3 tbsp. white sugar
- 1 large egg
- ¼ tsp. salt
- 1 cup buttermilk
- maple syrup
- ¼ cup vegetable oil

Directions:
1. Take the chicken and make slices of it.
2. Whisk together the flour, paprika, salt, pepper, and onion powder in a bowl.
3. Take another bowl and mix the egg, baking powder, baking powder and buttermilk.
4. Take one by one the chicken piece and dip it in the dry and then in the wet mixture.
5. Take the air fryer oven tray and spray it with the cooking spray.
6. Cook the pieces to 350°F for 6 minutes from both sides.
7. Drizzle the chicken pieces with honey and sprinkle paprika over them.
8. For waffles
9. Take the bowl and mix the cornmeal, sugar, baking powder and salt.
10. In another bowl, mix the egg, oil and buttermilk.
11. Whisk both mixtures together in a large bowl.
12. Take the waffle maker.
13. While chicken is cooking in the air fryer, start making the waffles.
14. Cook the waffles until golden brown.
15. Serve the waffles with honey on the top.

7. Cheesy Tater Tot Breakfast Bake

25 min | Easy | 2

Nutrition Facts
Per Serving: 385 calories; protein 20.2g; carbohydrates 16.7g; fat 28.8g; cholesterol 177.8mg; sodium 945.8mg.

Ingredients:
- 24 tater tots
- 5 sliced sausages
- 4 eggs
- ¼ cup sour cream
- 30ml milk
- 30g cheese
- 3 chopped onions
- Salt and pepper to taste
- Oil spray

Directions:
1. Coat the base of the fryer pan with oil.
2. Spread the sausage and tots in it.
3. Air fry the sausage and tots for 5-8 minutes.
4. Take a bowl and mix all remaining ingredients.
5. Add this mixture with fried sausage and tots in the air fryer and cook to 380° F for further 7-10 minutes.
6. Serve and enjoy.

8. Apple Fritters

20 min | Easy | 15

Nutrition Facts
Per Serving: 287 calories; protein 5.5g; carbohydrates 64.9g; fat 2.1g; cholesterol 48mg; sodium 238.1mg.

Ingredients:
- 1 ½ cup all-purpose flour
- 2 tsp. baking powder
- ¼ cup white sugar
- 1 ½ tsp. cinnamon (ground)
- ½ tsp. salt
- 2 eggs
- ⅔ cup milk
- 1 tbsp. lemon juice
- 1 ½ tsp. vanilla extract
- 2 peeled and chopped apples
- ¼ cup butter
- 1 cup brown sugar

Directions:
1. Take a bowl and mix sugar, flour, salt, cinnamon, and baking powder.
2. Now add milk, lemon juice, eggs and vanilla extract.
3. Add apples in batches.
4. Now put it in the air fryer oven tray and cook to 400° F for 2-3 minutes.
5. Melt the butter in a saucepan and add milk, sugar and vanilla extract. Mix it well and drizzle over the cooked patties.
6. Serve and enjoy.

Vegetable Recipes

1. Broccoli and Cheese Bake Potatoes

30 min   Medium   8

Nutrition Facts
Per Serving: 142 calories; protein 6.4g; carbohydrates 22.2g; fat 3.1g; sugars 2.6g; cholesterol 9.4mg; sodium 137.7mg

Ingredients:
- 4 medium potatoes
- 1 cup fat milk
- 2 tbsp. all-purpose flour
- ½ cup shredded cheese
- 1 cup chopped broccoli
- Chopped chives for garnishing

Directions:
1. Pierce the potatoes with a fork and microwave for 5-10 minutes. Flip and cook for further 5 minutes.
2. Heat the ¾ cup milk in a pan at medium heat.
3. Mix flour and remaining milk in a bowl until a smooth mixture is obtained.
4. Add the mixture of flour to the pan.
5. Bring a boil, whisk continuously.
6. Remove from the stove and add cheese. Stir until all the cheese is completely dissolved.
7. Add broccoli, cayenne and salt.
8. Cut the potatoes.
9. Layer the potatoes in the bucket of the air fryer oven and top with the broccoli mixture.
10. Add some cheddar.
11. Cook for 5-6 minutes.
12. Top with chives.
13. Serve and enjoy.

2. Veggie Quesadillas

38 min   Medium   5

Nutrition Facts
Per Serving: 39 calories; protein 1.4g; carbohydrates 3.5g; fat 2.4g; sodium 152.2mg.

Ingredients:
- ½ cup Pico de Gallo
- ¼ tsp. cumin
- 2 oz. Greek yogurt
- 1 cup black beans
- 1 cup bell pepper
- 2 tbsp. chopped
- 1 tsp. lime juice
- 1 tsp. lemon zest
- 1 cup zucchini
- 4 oz. cheddar cheese

Directions:
1. Place the dough and sprinkle 2 tablespoons ragged into the pan and ¼ cup each red pepper slice, zucchini slices and black beans.
2. Fold dough in the form of quesadillas and secure with toothpicks. Spray fryer oven basket with oil and cook at 400°F until golden brown and crispy, cheese is melted, and vegetables are softened turned over quesadillas through cooking.
3. While quesadillas cook, mix the yogurt and lime juice in a bowl. Cut each quesadilla into pieces.
4. Serve and enjoy it.

3. Buffalo Cauliflower Bites

25 min | Easy | 5

Nutrition Facts
Per Serving: 175 calories; protein 8.9g; carbohydrates 32.9g; fat 2g; cholesterol 0.2mg; sodium 1200.4mg.

Ingredients:
- 1 tsp. Salt
- 3 tbsp. dried parsley
- ½ cup Hot Sauce
- 2 tbsp. butter
- ½ tbsp. garlic powder
- ½ cup almond flour
- 1 tsp. olive oil
- 1 cauliflower

Directions:
1. Place cauliflower in a bowl.
2. Melt butter; mix in olive oil and sauce.
3. In another bowl, stick together almond flour, dry parsley, garlic powder and salt. Sprinkle the almond flour mixture over the cauliflower; gently mix it until everything is coated.
4. After that, transfer the half-prepared cauliflower to the fryer at 350°F for fifteen minutes. Cauliflower is done when the florets are a bit browned. Remove Cauliflower from the fryer; repeat the same procedure with the remaining cauliflower florets.

4. Vegetable Filled Empanadas

30 min | Medium | 5

Nutrition Facts
Per Serving: 39 calories; protein 1.4g; carbohydrates 3.5g; fat 2.4g; sodium 152.2mg.

Ingredients:

Dough
- 4 cups flour
- 1 ½ tsp. kosher salt
- 2 tsp. butter cold
- 1 ½ cup boiling water
- 3 tsp. shortening

Veggie filling
- 1 egg
- ¼ cup raisins
- 1 tomato
- 1 tsp. ground cumin
- 1 garlic clove
- 1 cup black beans
- ½ cup cilantro
- Half a bell pepper
- 1 gold potato
- 1 tsp. smoked paprika
- 1 onion
- 2 tsp. olive oil

Directions:
1. Place the dough and sprinkle 2 tablespoons ragged into the pan and ¼ cup each red pepper slice, zucchini slices and black beans.
2. Fold dough in the form of quesadillas and secure with toothpicks. Spray fryer oven basket with oil and cook at 400°F until golden brown and crispy, cheese is melted, and vegetables are softened turned over quesadillas through cooking.
3. While quesadillas cook, mix the yogurt and lime juice in a bowl. Cut each quesadilla into pieces.
4. Serve and enjoy it.

5. Bagel Kale Chips

30 min Medium 2

Nutrition Facts
Per Serving: 78 calories; protein 1.6g; carbohydrates 4.9g; fat 5.4g; sodium 258.7mg

Ingredients:
- ¼ tsp. poppy seeds
- 1 tsp. sesame seeds
- 1 tbsp. olive oil
- ½ tsp. minced garlic
- 1 tsp. soy sauce
- 6 cups kale leaves

Directions:
1. Wash and dry kale, leave and tear into one or one-half-inch pieces.
2. Mix all the ingredients in a bowl, rubbing the leaves until they are well coated with the mixture.
3. Place ⅓ of the leaves in the fryer basket and cook at 370°F.
4. Place kale chips on a baking sheet and sprinkle with seeds, garlic and poppy seeds. Repeat the same procedure with the remaining kale leaves.

6. Balsamic Brussels Sprouts

25 min Easy 5

Nutrition Facts
Per Serving: 157 calories; protein 4.6g; carbohydrates 15.9g; fat 8.8g; cholesterol 10.2mg; sodium 457.7mg.

Ingredients:
- Salt
- pepper to taste
- 1 tsp. balsamic vinegar
- 2 cups Brussels sprouts
- 1 tbsp. olive oil
- ½ cup red onions

Directions:
1. Add the Brussels sprouts and cut red onions to a bowl.
2. Spray with cooking oil and softening vinegar throughout. Sprinkle salt and pepper to taste. Spray the fryer with cooking oil.
3. Add the sprouts and onions, cook for 5 minutes at 350°F. Open the fryer and shake with tongs.

7. Vegan Lentils Sliders

20 min   Easy   4

Nutrition Facts
Per Serving: 272 calories; protein 15.2g; carbohydrates 43.1g; fat 6.2g; sodium 27.3mg.

Ingredients:
- 1 cup lentils
- 2 cup water
- ½ cup almond milk
- 1 tbsp. salt
- 1 tbsp. olive oil
- 1 cup croutons
- 1 tsp. pepper

Directions:
1. The lentil slider "dough" should be thick and slightly sticky.
2. Boil 1 cup lentils in 2 cups water for 10 min.
3. Blend the croutons and lentils in a blender. Also, add 1 tbsp. olive oil, ½ cup mill, 1 tsp. salt mix it thoroughly.
4. Roll the lentil dough into a small ball.
5. Place the foil in the air fryer basket and place the lentil slider ball on the foil
6. Set your air fryer to 350°F.
7. Cook it for 10 min in the air fryer.

8. Eggplant Parmesan

45 min   Medium   4

Nutrition Facts
Per Serving: 387 calories; protein 24.3g; carbohydrates 35.7g; fat 15.7g; cholesterol 134.6mg; sodium 1462.9mg.

Ingredients:
- ¼ cup grated mozzarella cheese
- parsley to taste
- 1 egg
- 1 tbsp. water
- 3 tbsp. grated parmesan cheese
- Salt to taste
- Olive oil spray
- 1 cup marinara sauce
- 1 tsp. Italian seasoning mix
- 3 tbsp. wheat flour
- 1 eggplant
- ½ cup bread crumbs

Directions:
1. Cut eggplant and rub some salt on it and leave it for at least fifteen minutes.
2. In a small bowl, mix egg with water and flour.
3. On a plate, combine bread crumbs, cheese, seasoning blend and salt.
4. Now apply to each eggplant slice and dip in the breadcrumb to coat it.
5. Preheat the fryer oven at 355°F. Then put the eggplant slices on a wire and cook for about 8 minutes.
6. Top the fried slices with one tablespoon of sauce and spread fresh mozzarella cheese on it.

9. Bagel Sticks

20 min   Easy   4

Nutrition Facts
Per Serving: 204 calories; protein 5.1g; carbohydrates 40.2g; fat 2.3g; sodium 700.2mg.

Ingredients:
- 1 cup self-rising flour
- 1 cup Greek yogurt
- 1 egg
- Poppy seeds and sesame seeds for topping

Directions:
1. Take a bowl, add yogurt and flour, mix it well to prepare the dough.
2. Take a cutting board, floured it, place dough on it, and cut it into fourths.
3. Roll dough by using your hand and make bagel shapes.
4. Take the bucket of air fryer, spray it with oil and place bagels in it. Brush it with egg wash.
5. Cook it at 330°F for 10 minutes.
6. Finally, place in tray sprinkle with poppy and sesame seeds and enjoy it!

10. Cheesecake Egg Roll Dupe

40 min   Medium   14

Nutrition Facts
Per Serving: 216 calories; protein 10.6g; carbohydrates 27g; fat 7.7g; cholesterol 24.8mg; sodium 627.9mg..

Ingredients:
- 1 tsp. cinnamon
- 2 tsp. butter
- 1 egg
- 8.5 oz. fig jam
- 1 tsp. lemon juice
- 16 oz. cream cheese
- ¼ cup sugar
- Olive oil
- 15 egg roll wrappers
- 1 tsp. vanilla extract
- 100g granulated sugar

Directions:
1. In a bowl of an electric mixer fitted, combine the cheese, sugar, juice and vanilla extract.
2. Mix on medium speed for 2 minutes, then remove cheesecake filling to a pastry bag.
3. Stir the jam till it can easily be scooped with a spoon.
4. Lay an egg roll wrapper and pipe on 2 tablespoons of cream cheese. Use a pastry brush with egg wash.
5. Fold in and spray egg rolls with olive oil.
6. Preheat fryer oven at 360°F for 10 minutes.
7. Place 5 egg rolls in the fryer basket. Fry for approximately 6 minutes.
8. Remove rolls from the basket and repeat frying of the egg rolls that are cooked. Combine sugar and cinnamon in a bowl and sprinkle over egg rolls.

Fish and Seafood Recipes

1. Catfish with Green Beans

25 min   Easy   2

Nutrition Facts
Per Serving: 426 calories; protein 32.6g; carbohydrates 28g; fat 17.7g; cholesterol 25.8mg; sodium 657.9mg.

Ingredients:
- 12 oz. green beans
- 1 tsp. brown sugar
- cooking spray
- ½ tsp. red pepper
- ⅜ tsp. salt
- 2 catfish fillets
- ¼ cup all-purpose flour
- 1 egg
- ⅓ cup panko
- ¼ tsp. black pepper
- 2 tbsp. mayonnaise
- 1 ½ tsp. chopped dill
- ⅗ tsp. dill relish
- ½ tsp. vinegar
- lemon wedges
- ⅛ tsp. granulated sugar

Directions:
1. Take the green beans into the air fryer, spray with cooking spray, and add salt, pepper, sugar, and red pepper. Cook for 10-12 minutes. Then transfer to a bowl and keep warm.
2. Toss the catfish with flour to coat it well. Then dip the coasted fish in eggs one by one. Then sprinkle it with panko.
3. Spray the fish with cooking spray. And place it in the air fryer. Cook to 400° F for 8-10 minutes and season with salt and pepper.
4. Mix mayonnaise, relish, dill, sugar and vinegar in a bowl.
5. Serve the beans and fish with lemon wedges and sauce.
6. Enjoy.

2. Fennel and Roasted Salmon

25 min   Easy   4

Nutrition Facts
Per Serving: 179 calories; protein 31.1g; carbohydrates 1.6g; fat 5.8g; cholesterol 72mg; sodium 1278mg.

Ingredients:
- 2 tsp. chopped parsley
- 1 tsp. chopped thyme
- 1 tsp. salt and pepper
- 4 skinless salmon fillets
- 2 tbsp. olive oil
- 4 cups sliced fennel
- ⅔ cup Greek yogurt
- 1 grated garlic clove
- 2 tbsp. orange juice
- 1 tsp. lemon juice
- 2 tbsp. chopped dill

Directions:
1. Take a small bowl and mix parsley, salt, pepper and thyme. Add some oil and sprinkle with a mixture of herbs.
2. Keep salmon fillets in the basket of the air fryer oven. And cook to 350° F for 8-10 minutes.
3. Take remaining ingredients in a bowl and toss well to mix.
4. Serve the fillets with fennel salad.
5. Enjoy.

3. Salmon Cake

25 min   Easy   2

Nutrition Facts
Per Serving: 320 calories; protein 25.5g; carbohydrates 3.6g; fat 21.7g; cholesterol 97.5mg; sodium 413.1mg.

Ingredients:
- 8 oz. salmon
- 1 egg
- ½ cup breadcrumbs
- 2 tbsp. chopped dill
- 2 tbsp. canola mayonnaise
- ¼ tsp. pepper/grinded
- 2 lemon wedges

Directions:
1. Drain the salmon. Take the salmon in a bowl.
2. Add all the ingredients and mix well.
3. Form small cake patties.
4. Place in the air fryer oven and cook at 400° F for 12-13 minutes.
5. Serve and enjoy.

4. Shrimp Spring Rolls with Sweet Chili Sauce

35 min   Easy   4

Nutrition Facts
Per Serving: 122 calories; protein 4.5g; carbohydrates 16.4g; fat 3.5g; cholesterol 8.9mg; sodium 154.7mg.

Ingredients:
- 2 ½ tbsp. sesame oil
- 2 cups shredded cabbage
- 1 cup carrots (chopped)
- 1 cup bell pepper
- 4 oz. peeled and chopped raw shrimp
- ¾ cup snow peas
- ¼ cup cilantro (chopped)
- 1 tbsp. lime juice
- 2 tsp. fish sauce
- ¼ tsp. red pepper
- 8 spring rolls
- ½ cup chili sauce

Directions:
1. Cook the vegetables in a skillet with some olive oil for 2-3 minutes and spread over the baking sheet.
2. Place the vegetable mixture, snow peas, shrimps, sauce in a bowl and drizzle with lime juice. Toss well to combine.
3. Take roll wrap and spoon the mixture over it. Fold the wrap to make the fine rolls. And brush with some oil.
4. Put these rolls in the air fryer and cook at 375°F for 8-10 minutes.
5. Serve with chili sauce.
6. Enjoy.

5. Fish Cake

20 min | Easy | 2

Nutrition Facts
Per Serving: 389 calories; protein3 4.5g; carbohydrates 26.4g; fat 3.5g; cholesterol 152.9mg; sodium 454.7mg.

Ingredients:
- 10 oz. white fish (chopped)
- ⅔ cup breadcrumbs
- 3 tbsp. cilantro (chopped)
- 2 tbsp. chili sauce
- 2 tbsp. canola mayonnaise
- 1 egg
- ⅛ tsp. salt and pepper
- 2 lime wedges

Directions:
1. Mix all the ingredients in a bowl.
2. Mix slam cake patties.
3. Place in the air fryer oven.
4. Spray with the cooking spray.
5. Cook at 400°F for 8-10 minutes.
6. Serve and enjoy.

6. Salmon with Horseradish Rub

30 min | Easy | 2

Nutrition Facts
Per Serving: 289 calories; protein 33.5g; carbohydrates 2.4g; fat 13.5g; cholesterol 72.9mg; sodium 534.7mg.

Ingredients:
- 2 grated horseradish
- 1 tbsp. parsley (chopped)
- 1 tbsp. capers (chopped)
- 1 tbsp. olive oil
- 12 oz. salmon fillets
- ¼ tsp. salt and pepper

Directions:
1. Mix horseradish, all spices and seasonings in a bowl.
2. Spread the mixture over the salmon.
3. Apply some cooking spray.
4. Place in the air fryer oven tray and cook at 375°F for 15-20 minutes.
5. Serve with the sauce.
6. Enjoy!

7. Chilean Sea Bass

30 min | Easy | 2

Nutrition Facts
Per Serving: 212 calories; protein 27.2g; carbohydrates 0.8g; fat 12.2g; cholesterol 77.9mg; sodium 227 mg.

Ingredients:
- ½ lb. Chilean sea bass
- 1 tsp. De Provence herbs
- 3 minced garlic cloves
- ⅓ cup white wine
- 3 tsp. olive oil
- Salt and pepper to taste
- 1 tsp. cayenne

Directions:
1. Mix all the ingredients in a bowl.
2. Rub the mixture over the fish to coat it.
3. Spray the air fryer with cooking spray.
4. Place the coated fish in it and cook to 375° F for 10-15 minutes.
5. Serve with sauce.
6. Enjoy.

8. Crab Cake

20 min | Easy | 4

Nutrition Facts
Per Serving: 547 calories; protein 15.4g; carbohydrates 55.4g; fat 33.7g; cholesterol 137.1mg; sodium 1214.5mg.

Ingredients:
- 8 oz. lump crab
- ¼ cup bell pepper (chopped)
- 2 onion (chopped)
- 2 tbsp. bread crumbs
- 2 tbsp. mayonnaise
- 1 tbsp. Dijon mustard
- 1 tsp. bay seasonings
- Oil spray
- 1 lemon juice

Directions:
1. Take all the ingredients in a bowl and mix well.
2. Form round patties.
3. Spray the bucket of air fryer oven with cooking spray and place the patties in it.
4. Cook for to 375°F 8–10 minutes.
5. Serve with sauce.
6. Enjoy.

9. Shrimp Fajitas

30 min   Easy   4

Nutrition Facts
Per Serving: 432 calories; protein 24.2g; carbohydrates 45.6g; fat 16.7g; cholesterol 172.6mg; sodium 1102.4mg.

Ingredients:
- 1 sliced red bell pepper
- 1 sliced green bell pepper
- 1 lb. uncooked shrimp
- 1 thin onion (sliced)
- 1 oz. fajita seasoning
- 3 tbsp. olive oil
- 4 toasted flour tortillas

Directions:
1. Take all the vegetables in a bowl and shrimp in a separate bowl.
2. Sprinkle the seasoning over the shrimp and mix well.
3. Drizzle oil on the vegetables and mix.
4. Drizzle olive oil in the shrimp.
5. Place the vegetables in the air fryer and cook to 400°F for 10-12 minutes.
6. Place the shrimps in the air fryer oven and cook to 400°F for 3-5 minutes.
7. Serve and enjoy.

10. Air Fryer Chili Lime Cod

20 min   Easy   2

Nutrition Facts
Per Serving: 247 calories; protein 161.4g; carbohydrates 2.4g; fat 1.7g; cholesterol 1.1g; sodium 494.5mg.

Ingredients:
- 1 tsp. powdered paprika
- 1 tsp. parsley
- 1 tsp. oregano
- ½ tsp. chili powder
- ½ tsp. garlic powder
- Cumin (grinded) to taste
- Black pepper
- ⅛ tsp. cayenne pepper
- 1 tbsp of olive oil
- 2 cods of fillets
- 1 lime zest

Directions:
1. Take all the spices in a bowl and mix.
2. Brush the fillets with oil and coat with a mixture of spices.
3. Refrigerate for 40 minutes.
4. Place the parchment paper in the air fryer oven and place the fillets in it.
5. Cook to 380° F for 10-13 minutes.
6. Remove from air fryer and sprinkle the lime zest over it.
7. Serve with sauce.
8. Enjoy.

Red Meat Recipes

1. Italian Style Meatball

30 min   Medium   8

Nutrition Facts
Per Serving: 93 calories; protein 7.6g; carbohydrates 2.2g; fat 6.1g; cholesterol 35.5mg; sodium 170.4mg.

Ingredients
- 2 lbs. beef
- 2 eggs
- 1 tsp. salt
- 1 cup milk
- 2 lbs. pork
- 1 cup Parmesan cheese
- ¼ cup parsley
- 1 tsp. black paper
- 2 cloves garlic
- 2 cup breadcrumbs

Directions:
1. Combine all the ingredients in a bowl and toss well.
2. Make equal size balls.
3. Place it in a single layer in the Air Fryer oven basket and cook at 400°F for 10-12 minutes.
4. The meatballs are done after 15 minutes.
5. Serve and enjoy it.

2. Pork Chops with Brussels Sprouts

25 min   Easy   6

Nutrition Facts
Per Serving: 194 calories; protein 19.2g; carbohydrates 8.1g; fat 9.2g; cholesterol 48.2mg; sodium 214.7mg

Ingredients:
- 1 tsp. mustard
- 6 oz. brussels sprouts
- 1 tsp. cooking oil
- 6 oz. pork chop
- 2 tsp. salt
- ½ tsp. black paper
- 1 tsp. maple syrup

Directions:
1. Firstly, marinate chops with cooking oil, salt and black pepper. Mix all ingredients oil, syrup, mustard, and remaining pepper in a bowl.
2. Add Brussels sprouts and toss them.
3. Place Chops on air fryer oven basket, and add Brussel sprouts. Heat air fryer oven at 400°F and cook for 20 minutes and cook it until golden color appears.

3. Cheesy Meat Filled Empanadas

39 min · Medium · 6

Nutrition Facts
Per Serving: 262 calories; protein 18.9g; carbohydrates 12.8g; fat 16g; cholesterol 82.5mg; sodium 772.8mg.

Ingredients:
- 1 lb. beef
- 2 tsp. garlic powder
- 2 tsp. black pepper
- ½ tsp. chili powder
- ½ tsp. cumin
- 20 -inch pie crusts
- ½ cup shredded cheddar cheese
- 1 tbsp. flour

Directions:
1. Brown the beef over medium heat.
2. Add garlic powder, black pepper, chili powder, and cumin when the beef is halfway cooked.
3. After the meat has cooled, cut the pie crusts into rings.
4. Sprinkle flour on the butter paper and roll out the pie crust.
5. Roll out the dough into a circle and cut out more circles.
6. Use one half of the pie crust circle to layer the cooled ground beef and shredded cheese.
7. To ensure that they are properly sealed. With a fork, crimp the folded edge.
8. Finally, apply the oil.
9. Preheat the air fryer oven to 350°F and cook for 8 minutes.
10. Serve with sour cream on the side.

4. Air Fryer Dumplings

30 min · Medium · 6

Nutrition Facts
Per Serving: 142 calories; protein 3.9g; carbohydrates 22.8g; fat 16g; cholesterol 2.5mg; sodium 272.8mg.

Ingredients:
- 6 oz. vegetable, chicken dumplings

Directions:
1. Preheat the air fryer oven to 370°F for 4 minutes.
2. Then, place the frozen dumplings in the air fry and spray with oil.
3. Cook for 5 minutes, shakes the basket.
4. Cook dumplings for another 4–6 minutes
5. Remove the air fryer dumplings from the basket and leaves them for 2 minutes before enjoying.

5. Air Fryer Steak

30 min   Medium   1

Nutrition Facts
Per Serving: 215 calories; protein 18.8g; carbohydrates 5.8g; fat 12.2g; cholesterol 55.3mg; sodium 202.5mg.

Ingredients:
- Rib piece 1 inch thick
- 2 tsp. olive oil
- 1 tsp. salt
- 2 tsp. black pepper
- Garlic herb butter as required
- 3 tsp. butter
- 1 tsp. garlic
- Fresh rosemary, thyme, and parsley

Directions:
1. The steak is marinated with olive oil, Italian seasoning, and salt pepper.
2. Add the steak to the air fryer oven and cook for 12 minutes, turning over after 6 minutes. Let the steak rest for 10 minutes and brush it with garlic butter.

6. BBQ Ribs

40 min   Medium   4

Nutrition Facts
Per Serving: 605 calories; protein 37.5g; carbohydrates 14.6g; fat 44.3g; cholesterol 165.5mg; sodium 405.1mg.

Ingredients:
- 8 Mutton ribs
- 3 tbsp. BBQ ribs sauce
- 1 cup BBQ sauce
- 1 tsp. salt
- 1 tsp. black paper

Directions:
1. Marinated the ribs with BBQ sauce, covering both sides of the ribs.
2. Cook for 20 minutes at 350°F in an air fryer oven.
3. Open the fryer oven and cover the ribs.
4. Remove and allow the ribs to rest for a few minutes.

7. Turkey Breast

60 min   Medium   10

Nutrition Facts
Per Serving: 253 calories; protein 41.2g; carbohydrates 0.4g; fat 10.1g; cholesterol 85.2mg; sodium 903.1mg.

Ingredients:

- 4 lb. turkey breast
- 1 tsp. olive oil
- 2 tsp. kosher
- ½ tbsp. Salt

Directions:

1. Place oil and salt all over the breast.
2. Preheat the air fryer oven to 350°F and cook each side for 20 minutes. Turn over the other side after 10 min.

8. Bacon Wrapped Jalapenos with Cream Sauce

18 min   Easy   8

Nutrition Facts
Per Serving: 203 calories; protein 12g; carbohydrates 2.5g; fat 16.7g; cholesterol 50.3mg; sodium 539.5mg.

Ingredients:

- 5 jalapeno peppers
- 1 cup cream cheese
- 2 tsp. dried parsley
- 1 tsp. onion powder
- 1 tsp. garlic powder
- 2 cup breadcrumbs
- 2 slices of bacon

Directions:

1. In a small bowl, mix the cream cheese, ½ of the breadcrumbs, and spices.
2. Mix well.
3. Fill the peppers with the mixture.
4. Wrap the pepper with bacon pieces.
5. Preheat your air fryer oven for 3 to 5 minutes at 370°F.
6. Cook in an air fryer at 370°F for 6-8 minutes.

9. Beef Empanadas

40 min   Medium   10

Nutrition Facts
Per Serving: 203 calories; protein 6g; carbohydrates 2.5g; fat 12.7g; cholesterol 30.3mg; sodium 179.5mg.

Ingredients:
- 2 tbsp. olive oil
- ½ onion chopped
- Salt as required
- 1 tbsp. Black paper
- 2 garlic cloves
- 1 lb. beef
- 1 tsp. cumin
- ½ cup green olives
- 1 egg

Directions:
1. In a pan, heat the oil, add the onion and garlic and cook for 4-5 minutes.
2. Toss the beef with the cumin in the skillet. Cook for around 10 minutes.
3. Add the olives and raisins and mix well.
4. Spoon beef mixture into the center of each empanada disc, one at a time. Fold the dough over the filling, and then press the edges of the dough together with the tines of a fork to seal it tightly. Rep with the remaining dough for empanadas.
5. Whisk together the egg and water in a small bowl. Brush the empanadas with the mixture
6. Spray your air fryer basket with cooking spray. Add as many empanadas as will fit in a single layer in your air fryer, usually 2-6 depending on the size.
7. Air fry for 8 minutes at 325°F.

10. Chili Boneless Buffalo Wings

28 min   Easy   8

Nutrition Facts
Per Serving: 689 calories; protein 29g; carbohydrates 33.7g; fat 42.9g; cholesterol 133.8mg; sodium 2324.5mg

Ingredients:
- 2 boneless chicken breasts pieces
- 2 cups flour
- 5 tsp. oil
- 3 tsp. salt
- 1 egg
- 1 cup milk
- ½ cup Frank's Buffalo Sauce
- 2 tbsp. butter
- 1 tsp. black pepper
- ½ tsp. cayenne
- ½ tsp. paprika

Directions:
1. In a bowl, make a mixture of flour and all spices.
2. In a separate bowl, whisk together egg and milk.
3. Cut chicken into 2 pieces.
4. Dip chicken pieces into egg/milk mix and then into flour mix again do chicken is double-coated
5. Cook in Air Fryer oven for 23 minutes at 150°F, flipping chicken after about 15 minutes.

11. Gingery Pork Meatballs

20 min   Easy   6

Nutrition Facts
Per Serving: 116 calories; protein 8.7g; carbohydrates 3.5g; fat 7.1g; cholesterol 31.1mg; sodium 381mg.

Ingredients:
- 3 garlic cloves
- 3 tbsp. cilantro
- 1 ½ lb ground pork
- 1 lb. ground beef meat
- 2 Eggs
- 1 lb Mushrooms
- Oil spray for air fryer basket

Directions:
1. Combine all the ingredients in a large bowl and mix it.
2. Making 24-28 meatballs
3. Spray coat the basket with oil. Add meatballs to the air fryer basket.
4. Cook in the air fryer oven for 8-12 minutes at 400°F.

12. Steak Fajitas

27 min   Easy   4

Nutrition Facts
Per Serving: 183 calories; protein 15.7g; carbohydrates 6.4g; fat 10.6g; cholesterol 24.2mg; sodium 1897.8mg

Ingredients:
- 1.5 lbs. steak sliced
- 1 cup pineapple juice
- 1 tbsp. lime juice
- 1 tbsp. olive oil
- ½ red bell
- ½ green bell
- 1 onion
- Salt as required
- Black pepper to taste
- 1 tbsp. soy sauce
- 1 garlic clove
- 1 tsp. chili powder
- 1 tsp. cumin
- 1 tsp. smoked paprika

Directions:
1. Combine minced garlic, pineapple juice, lime juice, olive oil, soy sauce, chili powder, cumin, and smoked paprika and keep it in the fridge for 5 hours.
2. Cover the base of the air fryer oven tray with foil and arrange onions and pepper in it.
3. Spray with oil and sprinkle with a little salt and pepper.
4. Cook at 400°F for 10 minutes. After 10 minutes, add steak pieces on top of peppers and cook at 400°F for 7 minutes.

1. Chicken Tender

35 min   Easy   4

Nutrition Facts
Per Serving: 637 calories; protein 73.6g; carbohydrates 83.5g; fat 5.1g; cholesterol 122.8mg; sodium 1161.5mg

Ingredients:
- 12 pieces chicken tenders
- 2 eggs
- 1 tsp. Salt
- Black pepper to taste
- ½ cup bread crumbs
- ½ cup panko (seasoned)
- Cooking spray (olive oil)
- Wedges of lemon

Directions:
1. Take a bowl to add chicken to it. Seasoned it with pepper and salt.
2. Take a deep bowl, add breadcrumbs and panko in it, and mix them.
3. Take another bowl, add eggs to it and beat them well.
4. Take chicken pieces, coat them with egg mixture, then dip into a mixture of bread crumbs remove the excess by shaking.
5. Place them in a tray and spray cooking spray on them.
6. Prepare the air fryer oven, preheat it at 400°F and cook the pieces for 5 to 6 minutes or until crispy.
7. Then take a dish, place cooked pieces in it, garnish with lemon pieces, finally serve and enjoy it!

2. Spicy Chicken Taquitos

45 min   Medium   6

Nutrition Facts
Per Serving: 176 calories; protein 11.3g; carbohydrates 12.9g; fat 8.2g; cholesterol 30.6mg; sodium 212.6m

Ingredients:
- 1 tsp. vegetable oil
- 2 tbsp. onion (diced)
- 1 clove of garlic (chopped)
- 2 tbsp. hot tomato sauce (Mexican style)
- 2 tbsp. green chili (chopped)
- 1 cup rotisserie chicken (shredded)
- 2 tbsp. Neufchatel cheese
- ½ cup Mexican cheese (shredded)
- 1 pinch salt
- 1 pinch of black pepper (grounded)
- 6 corn tortillas
- Cooking spray (avocado oil)

Directions:
1. Take a frying pan to add oil in it, add onions, then fry for 3 to 5 minutes or till softs, add garlic for one more mint. Then finally add Mexican tomato sauce and green chilies mix well.
2. Then add chess, chicken and cook it while stirring till cheese melts for approximately 3 minutes. Then sprinkle pepper and salt.
3. Take a frying fan heat tortilla in it. Add a spoon of chicken mixture to the center of each tortilla, then fold over and roll in the form of taquitos.
4. Prepare the air fryer oven to preheat it at 400°F.
5. Take a bucket of air fryer, place taquitos in it and spray them with cooking spray. Cook them for 6 to 10 minutes or till they turn golden. In halfway, turn the side and spray again with cooking spray and cook for another 3 to 5 minutes.
6. Finally, Serve and Enjoy It!

3. Hot Chicken Thigh

27 min   Easy   4

Nutrition Facts
Per Serving: 203 calories; protein 19.3g; carbohydrates 0.9g; fat 13.2g; cholesterol 70.9mg; sodium 355.2mg

Ingredients:
- 4 chicken thighs
- ½ tsp. Salt
- 1 tsp. paprika (smoked)
- 1 tsp. garlic powder
- ½ tsp. oregano
- ½ tsp. onion powder

Directions:
1. Prepare air fryer at 380°F for 5 minutes.
2. Take a large bowl, add chicken pieces in it, add salt, smoked paprika, oregano, garlic powder and onion powder and mix them well.
3. Spray the air fryer bucket with cooking spray, place chicken pieces in it, and cook them for 12 minutes.
4. While cooking turns the side of pieces and again cook for 10 more minutes. And cook till it becomes crispy.
5. Place the cooked pieces in place, then serve and enjoy it!

4. Fiesta Chicken Fingers

20 min   Easy   4

Nutrition Facts
Per Serving: 365 calories; protein 56g; carbohydrates 12.9g; fat 9.4g; cholesterol 231.3mg; sodium 1219.4mg

Ingredients:
- ¾ lb. chicken breasts (boneless)
- ½ cup buttermilk
- ¼ tsp. pepper
- 1 cup all purposes flour
- 3 cups corn chips (crushed)
- 2-pack taco (seasoning)
- Salsa or sour cream ranch dip sauce

Directions:
1. Prepare an air fryer to preheat it at 400°F.
2. Take chicken breast pound it with the help of a meat mallet in ½ inch thickness. Cut down into 1-in long strips.
3. Take a deep bowl and add pepper and buttermilk and mix it well.
4. Take 2nd deep bowl and add flour to it. Take 3rd bowl and add taco seasoning and corn chips in it and mix them well.
5. Take chicken pieces to dip one by one in flour mixture, then in buttermilk mixture, and finally coat them with tacos mixture.
6. Take a bucket of air fryer, place these coated pieces on its base, spray them with cooking spray, and cook for 7 -8 mints or until its coating becomes golden brown.
7. Finally, take a dish, place the cooked pieces in it, serve with dip sauce and enjoy it!

5. Quentin's Bourbon Peach Wings

35 min   Medium   4

Nutrition Facts
Per Serving: 65 calories; protein 5g; carbohydrates 6.9g; fat 3.4g; cholesterol 14.3mg; sodium 39.4mg

Ingredients:
- ½ cup peach
- 1 clove of garlic (chopped)
- 1 tbsp. brown sugar
- 2 tbsp. white vinegar
- 2 tbsp. bourbon
- 1 tsp. cornstarch
- 1 ½ tsp. water
- ¼ tsp. salt
- 2 lb. chicken wings

Directions:
1. Prepare an air fryer oven to preheat it at 400°F.
2. Take a food processor, add salt, garlic, brown sugar and preserves and blend them completely.
3. Take a frying pan, add the blended mixture in it, add vinegar and bourbon, then cook it and let it boil. Decrease the heat but again cook for 4 to 7 minutes till it becomes slightly thick.
4. Take a small bowl to add cornstarch and water till it becomes smooth. Add this to the preserve mixture and cook it for 1 to 2 minutes or thick. Save ¼ cup for serving purposes
5. Take a sharp knife, cut the joint of every wing remove the tips of wings.
6. Take the air fryer bucket, place the wings, cook for 6 to 7 minutes, turn its side, brush them with cooked sauce, and cook for 6 to 8 minutes or until the juices run.
7. Finally, take a dish, place the cooked wings in it, serve them with sauce and enjoy it!

6. Basil Pesto Chicken

20 min   Easy   2

Nutrition Facts
Per Serving: 773 calories; protein 65.5g; carbohydrates 63.7g; fat 35.1g; cholesterol 282.4mg; sodium 1806.3mg

Ingredients:
- 2 chicken thighs (boneless)
- 1-2 Roma tomatoes (cut in ¼ inch pieces)
- ¼ cup pesto sauce
- ⅓ cup mozzarella cheese (shredded)
- Black pepper
- ½ tsp. parsley flakes

Directions:
1. Take plastic wrap cover chicken thighs with it. Take some heavy material and place it on the chicken for flattening it.
2. Take aluminum foil and lined the surface of the air fryer with it.
3. Place the pieces of chicken thighs in the air fryer and sprinkle salt and pepper on them.
4. Take pesto sauce and spread on the chicken thighs, and on the top, add a layer of slices of tomatoes. Then cook them for 14 to 15 minutes at 360°F.
5. Then add a layer of cheese on tomato slices and cook them again for 4 to 5 minutes or until the meat temperature reaches 165°F.
6. Take a dish, place the cooked chicken thighs in it, sprinkle sparsely, then finally serve and enjoy it!

7. Tempero Baiano Brazilian Chicken

30 min   Medium   4

Nutrition Facts
Per Serving: 401 calories; protein 43.8g; carbohydrates 40.8g; fat 12.3g; cholesterol 178.8mg; sodium 535.4mg

Ingredients:
- 1 tsp. cumin seeds
- 1 tsp. oregano (dried)
- 1 tsp. parsley (dried)
- 1 tsp. turmeric
- 1 tsp. salt
- ½ tsp. coriander deeds
- ½ tsp. whole black peppercorns
- ½ tsp. cayenne pepper
- ¼ cup lime juice
- 2 tbsp. oil
- 1.5 lbs. chicken drumsticks

Directions:
1. Take a coffee grinder to add oregano, cumin, turmeric, parsley, kosher salt, coriander seeds, cayenne pepper, and peppercorns blend them.
2. Take a medium-sized bowl, add all the blended spices in it, and then add lime juice and oil. Take chicken drumsticks, coat them with this coating and marinate them for 30 minutes to 24 hrs.
3. For cooking, take a bucket of air fryer oven, place chicken pieces in it. Cook them for 20 to 25 minutes at 390°F.
4. Check the temp of chicken by using a meat thermometer and let it reach 1650F temp.
5. After that, place them in the dish, then serve and enjoy it.

8. Tandoori Chicken

45 min   Medium   3

Nutrition Facts
Per Serving: 346 calories; protein 36.6g; carbohydrates 12.7g; fat 17.8g; cholesterol 100.7mg; sodium 733.5mg

Ingredients:
- 6 chicken drumsticks
- ⅓ cup yogurt (plain)
- 1 tbsp. ginger paste
- 1 tbsp. garlic paste
- 1 tbsp. Kashmiri red chili powder
- ½ tsp. turmeric (ground)
- 1 tsp. garam masala
- 1½ tsp. salt
- 1 tbsp. fenugreek leaves (dried)
- 1 tbsp. lemon juice
- Cooking oil spray

Directions:
1. Take chicken drumsticks pat dry them using a paper towel. Remove the skin of the chicken.
2. Take a knife and make 2 to 4 cuts on the thick part of every drumstick.
3. Take a bowl to add ginger, yogurt, garlic, turmeric, salt, garam masala, and red chili powder. Then add fenugreek leaves after crushing them using your hands.
4. Then add chicken and lime juice, mix everything well, and place it for marination for about 20 to 30 minutes.
5. Prepare air fryer oven to preheat it at 350°F, take out the bucket of air fryer spray it with cooking spray.
6. Place the marinated chicken in its base and cook for 15 minutes. In halfway, turn the sides of pieces and spray with cooking spray.
7. Once the cooking is done, check the temperature of the chicken using a meat thermometer and let it reduce to 165°F.
8. Finally, place the cooked pieces in a tray, garnish them with lemon pieces, serve with mint chutney and enjoy it!

9. Pecan Crusted Chicken

35 min · Medium · 4

Nutrition Facts
Per Serving: 344 calories; protein 44.7g; carbohydrates 20.5g; fat 11g; cholesterol 93.9mg; sodium 562.7mg

Ingredients:
- 8 chicken tender breasts
- ½ cup mayonnaise
- 2 tbsp. whole grain mustard
- ½ cup pecans (finely chopped)
- 1 cup panko breadcrumbs
- ¼ cup parmesan cheese (finely grated)
- 2 tbsp. parsley (finely chopped)
- 1 pinch of pepper and salt

Directions:
1. Take chicken pieces to wash them, and pat dry using pepper tower, then sprinkle pepper and salt and place them on one side.
2. Take a bowl, add mayonnaise and mustard in it and mix it well.
3. Take another bowl, add breadcrumbs, pecans, parsley, and parmesan cheese to it.
4. Take pieces of chicken and one by one, coat them with mayonnaise mixture and then dip in a mixture of bread crumbs and remove excess by shaking.
5. Take a bucket of air fryer oven, place pieces in it, and cook them for 20 minutes at 360°F.
6. Finally, serve with dipping sauce and enjoy it!

10. Chicken Jalfrezi

17 min · Easy · 4

Nutrition Facts
Per Serving: 255 calories; protein 21.4g; carbohydrates 6.3g; fat 15.9g; cholesterol 78.4mg; sodium 744.5mg

Ingredients:
- 4 boneless, skinless chicken breasts cut into 2 or 3 pieces each
- 1 green pepper, deseeded and cut into rough 3cm chunks
- 1 onions chopped
- 2 tbsp olive oil
- 1/2 tsp Cayenne Pepper
- 1 tbsp garam masala
- 1 tsp ground turmeric
- 1 tsp sea salt
- 1/2 tsp Cayenne Pepper

For the Sauce
- 1/4 cup tomato sauce
- 1 tbsp water
- 1 tsp Garam Masala
- 1/2 tsp salt
- 1/2 tsp Cayenne Pepper

Directions:
1. Put in a large bowl, chicken, onions, peppers, oil, salt, turmeric, garam masala and cayenne and mix.
2. Place the chicken and vegetables in the air fryer basket.
3. Cook for 15 minutes to 350° F
4. Stir and toss half way through the cooking time.

For the sauce
1. In a small microwave safe bowl, combine tomato sauce, water, garam masala, salt, and cayenne.
2. Microwave on high for 1 minute. Remove and stir. Microwave some more. Set aside.
3. Once the chicken is cooked, remove and place chicken and vegetables in a large bowl and cover the chicken and vegetables evenly with the sauce.
4. Serve and enjoy it

11. Thai Peanut Chicken

35 min   Medium   4

Nutrition Facts
Per Serving: 350 calories; protein 23g; carbohydrates 40.4g; fat 10.3g; cholesterol 32.2mg; sodium 389.8mg

Ingredients:
- 1 lb. chicken thighs
- ¼ cup peanut butter
- 1 tbsp. sriracha sauce
- 1 tbsp. soy sauce
- 2 tbsp. Thai sweet chili sauce
- 2 tbsp. lime juice
- 1 tsp. garlic (chopped)
- 1 tsp. ginger (chopped)
- ½ tsp. salt
- ½ cup hot water
- ¼ cup cilantro (chopped)
- ¼ cup green scallions (chopped)
- 3 tbsp. peanuts (crushed)
- ½ cup hot water

Directions:
1. Take a bowl, add sriracha, soy sauce, peanut butter, sweet chili sauce, salt and lime juice, and mix them. Then add hot water to it mix it till it gives a smooth texture.
2. Take a zip lock bag to add chicken in it along with sauce; mix them well and marinate it for 30 minutes to 24 hours in the refrigerator.
3. After marination, place the chicken and coating in the bucket in the air fryer oven and cook them for 22 to 25 minutes at 350°F.
4. Place the cooked chicken in plate garnish with onions, peanuts, and cilantro serve with remaining sauce and enjoy it!

12. Turkish Chicken Kebab Taluk Shish

60 min   Medium   4

Nutrition Facts
Per Serving: 529 calories; protein 48.8g; carbohydrates 8.4g; fat 30.5g; cholesterol 176.3mg; sodium 1701.6mg

Ingredients:
- ¼ cup greek yogurt (full-fat)
- 1 tbsp. garlic (chopped)
- 1 tbsp. tomato paste
- 1 tbsp. vegetable oil
- 1 tbsp. lemon juice
- 1 tsp. salt
- 1 tsp. cumin (ground)
- 1 tsp. smoked paprika
- ½ tsp. cinnamon (ground)
- ½ tsp. black pepper (ground)
- ½ tsp. cayenne pepper
- 1 lb. chicken thighs (boneless skinless)

Directions:
1. Take a large bowl, add garlic, Greek yogurt, lemon juice, tomato paste, salt, oil, cumin, paprika, cinnamon, cayenne pepper, and black pepper mix, then well till the yogurt completely blends.
2. Take pieces of chicken, add them to the mixture and mix them well. Then marinate them for 30 minutes, for up to 24 hrs.
3. Take the bucket of air fryer oven, place the marinated chicken pieces in it in a single layer cook them for 10 minutes at 370°F.
4. Open the bucket of air fryer and flip the sides and again cook for 5 more minutes.
5. Check the temperature of the meat using a meat thermometer till it reaches 165°F. Then serve and enjoy it!

13. Tso's Chicken

35 min   Medium   4

Nutrition Facts
Per Serving: 460 calories; protein 32.8g; carbohydrates 22g; fat 27.5g; cholesterol 138.3mg; sodium 841.6mg

Ingredients:
- 1 lb. chicken thighs
- 1 egg
- ½ cup cornstarch
- ¼ tsp. salt
- ¼ tsp. white pepper (grounded)
- 7 tbsp. chicken broth
- 2 tbsp. soy sauce
- 2 tbsp. ketchup
- 2 tsp. sugar
- 1 ½ tbsp. canola oil
- 2 tsp. unseasoned rice vinegar
- 3–4 chiles de arbol
- 1 tbsp. ginger (chopped)
- 1 tbsp. garlic (chopped)
- 2 tbsp. green onions (thinly sliced)
- 1 tsp. sesame oil
- ½ tsp. sesame seeds

Directions:
1. Take a bowl, add egg and chicken, and mix them.
2. Taka, another bowl, adds the ⅓ cup cornstarch, pepper and salt and mix them. Then add chicken to this and mix them well for even coating.
3. Prepare an air fryer oven to preheat it at 400°F for 3 minutes, place chicken pieces in it, and cook them for 12 to 18 minutes.
4. Take a bowl, add broth in it and mix cornstarch in it; also, add soy sauce, sugar, ketchup, rice vinegar.
5. Take a frying pan, heat oil, and fry chilies on medium heat. Then add garlic and ginger again; cook for 30 to 40 seconds.
6. Take cornstarch broth mixture, whisk it again, pour in a frying pan; increase the heat to medium-high.
7. Add chicken to it when it starts boiling. Cook till the sauce becomes thick.
8. Transfer the cooked dish to a tray seasoned with green chili and sesame seeds; finally, enjoy it!

14. Chicken Wings Drumettes

20 min   Easy   4

Nutrition Facts
Per Serving: 488 calories; protein 18g; carbohydrates 20.8g; fat 37.5g; cholesterol 160.9mg; sodium 1783.3mg

Ingredients:
- 1lb. chicken wings
- 1 tbsp. olive oil
- 2 tsp. garlic salt
- 1 tsp. lemon pepper

Directions:
1. Take chicken pieces and pat dry them using a pepper towel.
2. Take a bowl, add chicken pieces in it, then add olive oil, garlic salt, lemon zest and mix them well.
3. Take a bucket of air fryer oven, place pieces of chicken in it, cook for 8 to 10 mints at 400°F on one side, turn aside, and cook again for 8 more minutes or till it becomes crispy.
4. Place the cooked pieces in the tray, then serve and enjoy!

Rotisserie Recipes

1. English Muffin Pizza

10 min   Easy   3

Nutrition Facts
Per Serving: 234 calories; protein 11.8g; carbohydrates 15.8g; fat 12.6g; cholesterol 34.5mg; sodium 770.5mg

Ingredients:
- 6 English muffins
- 15 oz. pizza sauce
- 4 oz. pepperoni
- Garlic powder
- Italian seasoning

Directions:
1. Cut the muffins in half.
2. Place them in the air fryer oven and cook to 390° F for 2-3 minutes.
3. Top with seasonings, spices and cheese.
4. Put them back in the air fryer and cook for 3-5 minutes.
5. Serve with sauce.
6. Enjoy.

2. Grilled Cheese Sandwiches

10 min   Easy   2

Nutrition Facts
Per Serving: 384 calories; protein 16g; carbohydrates 40g; fat 17.3g; cholesterol 45.5mg; sodium 1021.9mg

Ingredients:
- 4 slices of bread
- 1 tbsp. melted butter
- 1 and ½ oz. cheddar cheese

Directions:
1. Take the bread slices and apply butter.
2. Place the cheese slices on it and cover with another slice of bread.
3. Put the bread sandwiches in the air fryer and cook to 360° F for 2-3 minutes.
4. Serve and enjoy.

3. Hand Pies

20 min   Easy   6

Nutrition Facts
Per Serving: 718 calories; protein 9.5g; carbohydrates 80.1g; fat 41g; cholesterol 60.8mg; sodium 743.9mg

Ingredients:
- 4 tbsp. butter
- 2 diced apples
- 1 tsp. cinnamon
- ¼ cup brown sugar
- 1 tsp. cornstarch
- 1 tbsp. water
- 2 pie crusts (Refrigerated)
- 1 beaten egg
- 1 tbsp. water
- ½ cup powdered sugar
- Coarse sugar
- 2 tbsp. milk

Directions:
1. Melt the butter in a pan.
2. Add apples, sugar, and cinnamon.
3. Mix well till they are tendered.
4. Take a bowl and mix water and cornstarch.
5. Add it to the pan and cook till it thickens.
6. Roll out the crusts and cut them using a round-shaped bowl.
7. Whisk some water and egg in a bowl.
8. Spoon the apple mixture on the crusts and fold them.
9. Brush with the egg and water mixture.
10. Place in the air fryer oven and cook to 350° F for 9-10 minutes.
11. Mix the sugar and milk.
12. Take the pies out of the air fryer.
13. Apply the glaze using a brush and sprinkle some sugar.
14. Serve and enjoy.

4. Cheese Curds

35 min   Medium   4

Nutrition Facts
Per Serving: 126 calories; protein 6.9g; carbohydrates 4.5g; fat 10.5g; cholesterol 35.8mg; sodium 196.4mg.

Ingredients:
- 1 cup all-purpose flour
- 3 beaten eggs
- 2 cups bread crumbs
- 1 tsp. garlic powder
- ½ tsp. cayenne pepper
- 8 oz. cheese curds
- Cooking spray
- Dip sauce

Directions:
1. Take the flour in a bowl, beaten egg in another bowl, and crumbs mixed with spices in a 3rd bowl.
2. Coat the curds in flour, then dip in the beaten eggs and finally in the crumbs mixture.
3. Spray them with cooking spray and place them in the bucket.
4. Cook the curds for 4-5 minutes till they are crispy and brown.
5. Serve and enjoy.

5. Fried Pickles

20 min | Easy | 4

Nutrition Facts
Per Serving: 529 calories; protein 14.7g; carbohydrates 63.6g; fat 22.9g; cholesterol 87.4mg; sodium 3292.2mg

Ingredients:
- 30 dill pickles
- ½ cup flour
- ½ tsp. salt and pepper
- 2 eggs
- 2 tbsp. pickle juice
- ½ tsp. garlic powder
- ⅓ cup bread crumbs
- Oil spray

Directions:
1. Mix the flour, seasoning, salt in a bowl. Take crumbs in another bowl.
2. Beat the eggs with pickle juice in a 3rd bowl.
3. Now take the pickles, coat them with the flour, dip them in the egg mixture, and finally in the crumbs.
4. Spray the air fryer with the cooking spray.
5. Place them in the air fryer and cook to 350° F for 8-10 minutes.
6. Serve with the dipping sauce.
7. Enjoy.

6. Browned Blooming Onions

45 min | Easy | 4

Nutrition Facts
Per Serving: 131 calories; protein 0.8g; carbohydrates 7g; fat 11.6g; cholesterol 30.5mg; sodium 83.7mg.

Ingredients:
For Onions
- 1 onion
- 3 eggs
- 1 tsp. garlic powder
- 1 tsp. powdered onion
- 1 cup bread crumbs
- 2 tsp. paprika
- Salt to taste
- 3 tbsp. olive oil

For sauce
- ⅔ cup mayonnaise
- ½ tsp. paprika
- 2 tbsp. ketchup
- 1 tsp. horseradish
- ½ tsp. garlic powder
- ¼ tsp. dried oregano
- Salt

Directions:
1. Slice the onions.
2. Take a bowl and whisk egg and some water.
3. Take another bowl and mix the spices and crumbs.
4. Dip the onions in eggs and then in the crumbs mixture.
5. Spray the air fryer oven with cooking spray.
6. Place the onions in it and cook to 400°F for 15-20 minutes.
7. Serve with the sauce.
8. Enjoy.

7. Crunch Taco Bells

30 min   Easy   4

Nutrition Facts
Per Serving: 328 calories; protein 15.6g; carbohydrates 22.8g; fat 0.4g; cholesterol 45.1mg; sodium 971.4mg

Ingredients:
- 1 lb. beef
- 2 tbsp. taco seasoning
- 2 tsp. cumin
- ⅓ cup water
- ½ cup nacho cheese
- 4 shells of tostada
- 1 diced tomato
- ½ cup sour cream
- Oil spray
- Tortillas

Directions:
1. Cook the beef in a pan until it is browned and drain off the excess water.
2. Season it with cumin, garlic powder and other spices. Mix well.
3. Add some water and again cook at low heat and allow it to simmer until it thickens.
4. Take the tortilla and put the mixture over it. Cover with another tortilla.
5. Spray the air fryer with cooking spray.
6. Place it in the air fryer oven and cook to 400°F for 4-5 minutes.
7. Serve and enjoy.

8. Texas Roadhouse Fried Pickles

25 min   Easy   1

Nutrition Facts
Per Serving: 367 calories; protein 4.3g; carbohydrates 2533g; fat 25.7g; cholesterol 10mg; sodium 1025.4mg.

Ingredients:
- 2 cups sliced pickles
- 1 cup flour
- 1 tbsp. garlic powder
- 1 tbsp. Cajun seasonings
- ½ tbsp. cayenne pepper
- Cooking spray

Directions:
1. Mix the spices and flour in a bowl.
2. Coat the pickles with a flour mixture.
3. Spray the air fryer with cooking spray.
4. Place the coated pickles in it and cook to 400° F for 5-10 minutes.
5. Serve with sauce.
6. Enjoy.

Appetizers and Snacks Recipes

1. Banana Bread

60 min   Medium   8

Nutrition Facts
Per Serving: 192 calories; protein 7.9g; carbohydrates 31g; fat 4.4g; cholesterol 0.5mg; sodium 1861mg.

Ingredients:
- ¾ cup all-purpose flour
- 1 tsp. cinnamon grounded
- 4 tsp. baking soda
- 2 pieces bananas (mashed)
- 2 eggs (beaten)
- ½ tsp. salt
- ½ cup sugar
- 2 tbsp. oil (vegetable)
- ½ cup whole milk
- Cooking oil spray
- ½ tsp. vanilla extract
- 2 tbsp. walnuts (crushed)

Directions:
1. Prepare Air fryer oven and preheat it to 310°F.
2. Take a cake pan of 6-inches and coat the base of it with cooking oil spray.
3. Take cinnamon, flour, baking soda and salt in a bowl and blend them.
4. Take another bowl and mix egg, bananas, oil, vanilla extract and sugar in it.
5. Now mix the above 2 prepared mixtures completely.
6. Then pour the prepared mixture into the prepared cake pan and decorate its surface by sprinkling crushed walnuts.
7. Place the prepared cake pan in the preheated air fryer for approximately 30 minutes. (Use the toothpick for testing either cake is prepared or not).
8. Finally, take a wire rack and transfer cooked bread on it and let it cool down for 15 to 20 minutes.
9. After that, take out the delicious bread from the pan, serve it and enjoy it!

2. Churros with Chocolate Sauce

80 min   Difficult   12

Nutrition Facts
Per Serving: 681 calories; protein 3.5g; carbohydrates 56.1g; fat 50.1g; sodium 283.1mg

Ingredients:
- ¼ tsp. salt
- ½ cup water
- ½ cup butter
- 2 tsp. cinnamon (grounded)
- ⅓ cup sugar
- 4 oz. baking chocolate (chopped finely)
- 2 tbsp. vanilla kefir
- 3 tbsp. heavy cream

Directions:
1. Take a small saucepan, mix salt, water and ¼ cup butter in it and boil it on medium-high flame.
2. Decrease the heat from medium-high to medium-low and mix it vigorously by adding flour in it with the help of a wooden spoon until the dough becomes flat and smooth.
3. Keep repeating the process of stirring for 2 to 3 minutes until the dough starts to separate away from the pan's side surface and the dough makes the film on the bottom surface of the pan.
4. Take a medium-sized bowl, transfer the prepared dough in it, and let it cool for approximately one minute.
5. After it cools down, add eggs in it one by one with continuous stirring until the dough becomes completely smooths.
6. Take a piping bag with a medium-size star-shaped tip, add this prepared mixture to it, and place it in the fridge for 30 minutes.
7. Prepare the air fryer to 380°F.
8. Cut the 3 inches long 6 pipe shape pieces of the chilled mixture and place them in the bucket of air fryer in a single layer and cook them for 10 minutes.
9. Keep repeating the process for the remaining mixture.
10. Take a bowl and mix the cinnamon and sugar in it.
11. Take the cooked churros out of the air fryer, let them cool for a while and after that, coat them with the remaining melted butter and coat them with the cinnamon-sugar mixture by rolling them in it.
12. Take a small bowl, put cream and chocolate in it and microwave them until it melts.
13. Finally, serve the deliciously prepared Churros with the chocolate sauce and Enjoy It!

3. Strawberry Pop-Tarts

120 min   Difficult   6

Nutrition Facts
Per Serving: 313 calories; protein 2.8g; carbohydrates 25.5g; fat 23.3g; cholesterol 60 mg; sodium 226.5mg.

Ingredients:
- ¾ cup strawberries
- ¼ cup sugar (Grounded)
- 14 oz. piecrusts (refrigerated)
- 1 ½ tsp. lemon juice
- 1 tbsp. sprinkles
- ½ cup powdered sugar
- Cooking oil spray

Directions:
1. Take a medium-size bowl, mix the strawberries and grounded sugar in it, keep it for 15 minutes, with occasional mixing.
2. Microwave them for 10 minutes on a high setting, stirred them halfway while cooking and keep cooking until mixture size reduces and becomes shiny.
3. After 10 minutes, place it out of the microwave and cool it for approximately 30 minutes.
4. Floured a surface and roll the pie crust over it into a circle of 12 inches.
5. After that, cut down the rolled dough into 12 rectangular shape pieces.
6. Put the 2 tsp. a prepared strawberry mixture in the center of each rectangular piece (leave ½ inch border from all sides).
7. Now brush the edges of the filled rectangular piece with water and place the other piece on it and press the edges with a fork. Then coat the surface with cooking spray.
8. Take the air fryer oven tray, place the 3 prepared tarts in it (single layer), and cook it until its color becomes golden brown or approximately 10 minutes at 350°F.
9. Repeat this whole process with other tarts also.
10. After that, let them cool for about 30 minutes by placing them wire rack.
11. Take a bowl, mix the lemon juice and powdered sugar in it. Coat this on the cooked tarts and then sprinkle the colorful candy sprinkles on them and enjoy it!

4. Loaded Baked Potatoes

25 min   Easy   2

Nutrition Facts
Per Serving: 301 calories; protein 11.6g; carbohydrates 33.8g; fat 15.3g; cholesterol 27.3mg; sodium 549.2mg.

Ingredients:
- 11 oz. potatoes
- 2 bacon slices (center cut)
- 2 tsp. olive oil
- 1 ½ tbsp. chives (chopped)
- ½ oz. cheddar cheese low fat (finely shredded)
- 2 tbsp. low-fat sour cream
- ⅛ tsp. salt

Directions:
1. Coat potatoes with oil, place them in a tray of air fryer oven and cook them at 350°F for 25 minutes, and keep stirring them.
2. On the other side, take a medium-sized frying pan and cook bacon in it for 7 minutes or until they become crispy over a medium flame.
3. Now remove the crispy cooked bacon from the pan and crush them.
4. Take a serving dish and place the air-fried potatoes in it. Sprinkle the crushed bacon on them.
5. Add the remaining topping that is cheese, sour cream, salt, chives, and remaining crushed bacon. Finally, serve and enjoy it!

5. Toasted Eggplant

15 min   Easy   6

Nutrition Facts
Per Serving: 54 calories; protein 2.4g; carbohydrates 3.2g; fat 3.7g; cholesterol 3.9mg; sodium 71.7mg

Ingredients:
- 2 eggs
- ½ cup wheat germ (toasted)
- ½ cup parmesan cheese
- 1 eggplant (medium size)
- ¾ tsp. garlic salt
- 1 tsp. Italian seasoning
- 1 cup pasta sauce meatless (warmed)
- Cooking spray

Directions:
1. Prepare the air fryer oven by preheating it at 375°F.
2. Take a deep bowl, Wisk eggs in it, and mix the wheat germ, cheese, and seasonings.
3. Take the eggplant and trim its ends; after that, cut it lengthwise into ½ inch long thick pieces. After that, cut each slice into ½ inch strips.
4. Dip these strips into eggs and then coat them with a mixture of cheese.
5. Take the air fryer bucket, arrange the coated strips, spray cooking spray, and arrange them in a single layer on its surface.
6. Cook these strips for 4 to 5 minutes or until it's golden brown.
7. Repeat this with all pieces and then finally serve them immediately with the pasta sauce and enjoy it!

6. Peach Hand Pies

60 min   Medium   8

Nutrition Facts
Per Serving: 415 calories; protein 3.5g; carbohydrates 55g; fat 21.7g; cholesterol 15.3mg; sodium 279.6mg.

Ingredients:
- 5 oz. peaches (chopped and peeled)
- 1 tbsp. lemon juice
- 3 tbsp. sugar (grounded)
- 1 tsp. vanilla extract
- 1 tsp. cornstarch
- ¼ tsp. salt
- Cooking spray
- 1 oz. Pie crust (refrigerated)

Directions:
1. Take a medium bowl, add lemon juice, chopped peaches, vanilla extract and sugar in it and mix them properly; keep it for 15 to 20 minutes and keep on stirring after 2 to 3 minutes.
2. Now drain the peaches and keep the 1 tbsp. liquid. Add the cornstarch to this liquid and mix them.
3. After that, cut the 8 circular pieces of pie crusts. Add the filling in the center of every circle. Water the edges of every piece and fold them over the filling, making a half-moon shape. Press the edges with a fork for sealing it and finally, make 3 cuts on the top of every pie and spray them with cooking spray.
4. Now place the single layer of pies in the air fryer oven tray and let them cook for 12 to 15 minutes at 350°F.
5. Do this with all other remaining pies and then serve and enjoy it!

7. Tasty Calzone

25 min | Medium | 16

Nutrition Facts
Per Serving: 275 calories; protein 12.3g; carbohydrates 34.2g; fat 10.1g; cholesterol 29mg; sodium 613.5mg

Ingredients:
- All purposes flour
- 1 lb. pizza dough
- 1 cup pizza sauce
- 8 oz. mozzarella cheese (shredded)
- 6 oz. pepperoni (thin slices)

Directions:
1. Roll the pizza dough on a floured surface till it becomes ¼ inch thick.
2. Cut the 8 to 10 round dough shapes with the help of a glass or a 3-inch cutter; with the remaining dough, reroll it and repeat the same process and make more round shape dough circles.
3. Take a baking tray with a baking sheet and transfer the round cut pieces onto it.
4. Now top every circle with 2 tsp. the pizza sauce, 1 tbsp. cheese and 1 tsp. pepperoni. Now fold the corner of the dough and seal the edges by using a fork.
5. Prepare the air fryer oven at 375°F and start frying in a group of 4; cook them for 8 minutes or till they become golden brown.
6. Serve the baked calzones with pizza sauce and enjoy it!

8. Mexican Style Corn

20 min | Easy | 4

Nutrition Facts
Per Serving: 302 calories; protein 5.3g; carbohydrates 18.2g; fat 22.7g; cholesterol 8.6mg; sodium 316.2mg

Ingredients:
- 4 fresh corn pieces
- 1 ½ tbsp. unsalted butter
- 2 tsp. garlic (chopped)
- 1 tsp. lime zest
- 1 tbsp. fresh lime juice
- ½ tsp. salt
- Cooking spray
- ½ tsp. black pepper
- 2 tbsp. cilantro (chopped)

Directions:
1. Take the corn cobs, coat them with cooking spray.
2. Prepare the Air fryer oven at 400°F, place the single layer of prepared cobs in the fryer bucket, cook them for 15 minutes, and keep the cobs turning in the middle of cooking.
3. Take a small bowl and mix butter, lime zest, lime juice and garlic in it.
4. Microwave this mixture on a High setting till the butter melts for about 30 sec.
5. Take a serving dish place the prepared cobs on the plate. Pour the mixture of butter on cobs and sprinkle salt and pepper along with the cilantro.
6. Serve immediately and enjoy it!

9. Sweet Potato Fries

20 min   Easy   2

Nutrition Facts
Per Serving: 401 calories; protein 4.3g; carbohydrates 53.7g; fat 152g; sodium 632.9mg

Ingredients:
- 1 sweet potato
- 1 tbsp. canola oil
- ½ tsp. salt
- ¼ tsp. pepper
- ⅛ tsp. sweet paprika (grounded)
- ⅛ tsp. garlic powder
- 1 sweet potato

Directions:
1. Take the sweet potato peel and cut it into ½ inch wide fries' slices
2. Preheat the air fryer oven to 400°F.
3. Take a bowl, mix the sweet potatoes, fries and canola oil in it, and then add pepper, salt, garlic powder and paprika in it and mix completely for smooth and equal coating.
4. Take the sweet potatoes fries and divide them into 3 to 4 equal portions for cooking. In the bucket of air fryer, place the even layer of potatoes and cook them for 10 to 12 minutes. Repeat this process with other batches.
5. Serve and enjoy it!

10. Whole Wheat Pita Pizza

15 min   Easy   2

Nutrition Facts
Per Serving: 185 calories; protein 5.1g; carbohydrates 30.1g; fat 5.0g; sodium 98.7mg

Ingredients:
- ¼ cup marinara sauce
- 1 cup spinach leaves
- 2 whole-wheat pita
- 1 plum tomato (cut into 8 pieces)
- 1 garlic clove (thinly sliced)
- ¼ cup mozzarella cheese (pre-shredded)
- ¼ oz. parmigiano-reggiano cheese

Directions:
6. On each side of pita bread, spread marinara sauce.
7. Add topping of tomato slices, spinach leaves, garlic and cheese.

Cook the prepared and topped pita bread one by one in the air fryer oven at 350°F for 5 to 6 minutes. Serve and enjoy it!

Delicious Dessert Recipes

1. Nutella Banana Sandwich

8 min   Easy   2

Nutrition Facts
Per Serving: 722 calories; protein 7.1g; carbohydrates 101.4g; fat 34.5g; cholesterol 78.5mg; sodium 314.2mg.

Ingredients:
- Butter as required
- ¼ cup Nutella spread of the choice
- 4 bread slices
- 1 banana

Directions:
1. Spread butter over one of the bread slices.
2. Spread Nutella over the other slice of the bread.
3. Place banana slices over one of the bread pieces.
4. Cover the first bread piece with the second one to make a sandwich.
5. Place the sandwich in the preheated air fryer oven at 375°F for 4 minutes.
6. Change the side and again, and cook for 3 more minutes.
7. Serve and enjoy it.

2. Chocolate Chip Cookies

30min   Medium   4

Nutrition Facts
Per Serving: 188 calories; protein 2g; carbohydrates 24.7g; fat 9.8g; cholesterol 28.7mg; sodium 178.6mg.

Ingredients:
- 2 sticks of butter (unsalted)
- ¾ cup sugar (granulated)
- 1 tbsp. vanilla extract
- 2 eggs
- 1 tsp. salt
- ¾ cup sugar
- 1 tsp. baking soda
- 2 ⅓ cups all-purpose flour
- 2 cups chocolate chips
- ¾ cup walnuts (chopped)
- Cooking spray

Directions:
1. Take a bowl of a stand mixer, add butter, and mix it till it becomes soft.
2. Add sugar and brown sugar mix again on a medium setting for 3 to 4 minutes.
3. Take vanilla extract, eggs and salt, add in bowl mixture mix them well. Then add flour, finally add walnuts and chocolate chips, then mix them again using a rubber spatula.
4. Prepare an air fryer oven to preheat it at 350°F for 5 minutes.
5. Take a bucket of air fryer lined its surface with parchment pepper place 2 tbsp. of the mixture on the tray, press them genteelly for making cookie shape cook for 5 minutes or till golden brown.
6. Remove from oven, let it still for a while, finally serve and enjoy it!

3. Buttermilk Biscuits

12 min   Easy   10

Nutrition Facts
Per Serving: 402 calories; protein 8.2g; carbohydrates 50.2g; fat 17.2g; cholesterol 2.5mg; sodium 907mg

Ingredients:
- 2 ½ cups all-purpose flour
- ½ tsp. baking soda
- 1 ½ tbsp. baking powder
- 1 tsp. sugar
- 1 tsp. salt
- ½ cup butter (unsalted)
- 1 cup buttermilk (chilled)

Directions:
1. Take a bowl, add dry ingredients to it mix them well.
2. Take cubes of butter using your hand; break them mix in flour till they become pea-sized.
3. Take buttermilk, pour this in flour-butter mixture mix them well.
4. Take out the dough from the bowl, place it on a floured surface, dice it into ¾ inch thick. Cut biscuit shapes using a biscuit cutter.
5. Place these in an air fryer oven tray and cook for 13-15 minutes at 325°F for 13 to 15 minutes.
6. Finally, serve with honey, butter, or any jam and enjoy it!

4. Chocolate Chip Oatmeal Cookies

20 min   Easy   6 dozen

Nutrition Facts
Per Serving: 238 calories; protein 3.1g; carbohydrates 30.1g; fat 12.8g; cholesterol 28.6mg; sodium 132.8mg

Ingredients:
- 1 cup softened butter
- ¾ cup sugar
- ¾ cup brown sugar
- 2 eggs
- 1 tsp. vanilla extract
- 3 cups cooking oats
- 1 ½ cup all purposes flour
- 1 pack vanilla pudding
- 1 tsp. baking soda
- 1 tsp. salt
- 2 cups chocolate chips (semisweet)
- 1 cup chopped nuts

Directions:
1. Prepare an air fryer oven to preheat it at 325°F.
2. Take a bowl, add cream, butter and sugars mix them till they become fluffy or for 5 to 7 minutes. Add egg and vanilla mix again
3. Take another bowl, add flour, dry pudding mix, whisk oats, baking soda and salt; gradually beat into the creamed mixture, then add nuts and chocolate chips.
4. Take a spoon, add drops of the mixture on the sheet, and spread it. Cook till light brown or for 8 to 10 minutes.
5. Finally, serve and enjoy it!

5. Mini Nutella Donuts Holes

30 min   Medium   32 donuts

Nutrition Facts
Per Serving: 316 calories; protein 5.3g; carbohydrates 52.4g; fat 10.5g; cholesterol 54.2mg; sodium 437.9mg.

Ingredients:
- 1 egg
- 1 tbsp. water
- ⅔ cup Nutella
- 1 tube flaky biscuits (refrigerated)
- Confectioner sugar

Directions:
1. Prepare an air fryer oven to preheat it at 300°F temperature.
2. Take biscuits on a floured surface and roll them in a 6-inch-thick sheet, then cut into circles.
3. Take egg wash, brush it on biscuits surface add 1 tsp. Nutella seal it by pinching all corners together at one spot.
4. Place in air fryer cook for 8 to 10 minutes or till golden brown.
5. Finally, serve and enjoy it!

6. Delicious Bread Pudding

25 min   Easy   6

Nutrition Facts
Per Serving: 348 calories; protein 6.3g; carbohydrates 37.1g; fat 19.3g; cholesterol 254.5mg; sodium 261.1mg

Ingredients:
- 2 cups bread (cubes)
- 1 egg
- ⅔ cup heavy cream
- ½ tsp. vanilla extract
- ¼ cup sugar
- ¼ cup chocolate chips

Directions:
1. Take baking dish spray with cooking spray. Place bread cubes in it sprinkle chocolate chips on it.
2. Take a bowl, add egg, vanilla extract, whipped cream, and sugar; mix them well.
3. Take this mixture to pour on bread cubes; cook for 15 minutes at 350-degree°F temperature.
4. Finally, serve and enjoy it!

7. Greek Bread Sticks

20 min   Easy   32

Nutrition Facts
Per Serving: 200 calories; protein 6.2g; carbohydrates 40.4g; fat 0.8g; cholesterol 13.7mg; sodium 204.3mg.

Ingredients:
- ¼ cup artichoke hearts
- 2 tbsp. pitted Greek olives
- 1 pack puff pastry frozen
- 1 carton of artichoke cream cheese and spreadable spinach
- 2 tbsp. parmesan cheese grated
- 1 egg
- 1 tbsp. water
- 2 tsp. sesame seeds
- tzatziki sauce (Refrigerated)

Directions:
1. Prepare an air fryer oven to preheat it at 325°F.
2. Take a food processor to add olive and artichokes, chop them well.
3. Take a pastry sheet, place it on the floured surface, take cream cheese spread over it, then add a half mixture of artichoke.
4. Drizzle cheese and fold it and press gently for sealing.
5. Take egg wash, brush it on pastry sprinkle sesame seeds on it. Then cut these rectangles into ¾ inch strips and twist them.
6. Finally, cook them for 12 to 15 minutes.
7. Serve and enjoy it!

8. Carrot Coffee Cake

35 min   Medium   6

Nutrition Facts
Per Serving: 615 calories; protein 6.1g; carbohydrates 83.4g; fat 30.1g; cholesterol 70.2mg; sodium 540.1mg

Ingredients:
- 1 egg
- ½ cup buttermilk
- ⅓ cup + 2 tbsp. sugar
- 3 tbsp. canola oil
- 2 tbsp. dark brown sugar
- 1 tsp. grated orange zest
- 1 tsp. vanilla extract
- ⅔ cup all-purpose flour
- ⅓ cup white wheat flour
- 1 tsp. baking powder
- 2 tsp. pumpkin pie spice
- ¼ tsp. baking soda
- ¼ tsp. salt
- 1 cup carrots (shredded)
- ¼ cup cranberries (dried)
- ⅓ cup walnuts (toasted and chopped)

Directions:
1. Prepare an air fryer oven to preheat it to 350°F.
2. Take 6-inch baking pan grease and flour it.
3. Take a bowl and whisk egg, ⅓ cup sugar, buttermilk, oil, orange zest, brown sugar, and vanilla and mix them well.
4. Take another bowl and whisk flours, baking soda, baking powder, pumpkin pie spice, and salt; mix them well. Add this in a mixture of eggs. Take carrots and cranberries, fold them then pour into the baking pan.
5. Take a small bowl, add walnuts, remaining 1 tsp. Pumpkin spice and remaining 2 tbsp. Sugar. Pour on the batter and cook for 35 to 40 minutes.
6. Finally, serve and enjoy it!

9. French Toast Cup with Raspberries

40 min   Medium   2

Nutrition Facts
Per Serving: 344 calories; protein 12.2g; carbohydrates 30.1g; fat 19.2g; cholesterol 221.1mg; sodium 516.5mg

Ingredients:
- 2 eggs
- 2 Italian bread slices
- ½ cup raspberries (frozen)
- 2 oz. cream cheese
- 2 large eggs
- ½ cup milk
- 1 tbsp. maple syrup

For preparing a raspberry syrup
- 2 tsp. cornstarch
- ⅓ cup water
- 2 cups raspberries (frozen)
- 1 tbsp. lemon juice
- 1 tbsp. maple syrup
- ½ tsp. grated lemon zest
- Cinnamon ground

Directions:
1. Take bread cut into cut divide them into 2 greased cups.
2. Take raspberries and cheese sprinkle on it add remaining bread.
3. Take a bowl, add egg, milk and maple syrup; mix them well. Refrigerate for 1 hour.
4. Prepare air fryer oven to preheat at 325°F. Place bread cups cook for 12 to 15 minutes.
5. Take a frying pan, add water and cornstarch, mix them, then add raspberries, syrup, lemon juice and zest; cook it till boils decrease heat. Cook for 2 minutes more; finally, strain this and remove seeds from it, set aside, and let it cool.
6. Finally, serve this with toast cups and enjoy it!

10. Chocolate Zucchini Bread

30 min   Medium   8

Nutrition Facts
Per Serving: 275 calories; protein 3.2g; carbohydrates 34.7g; fat 15.1g; cholesterol 27.4mg; sodium 190.6mg

Ingredients:
- 2 tbsp. vegetable oil
- ½ cup all-purpose flour
- ¼ tsp. salt
- ¼ cup cocoa powder
- 2 tbsp. butter
- ½ tsp. baking soda
- 1 egg
- 6 tbsp. sugar
- ¾ cup zucchini shredded
- ½ tsp. vanilla extract
- ½ cup chocolate chips

Directions:
1. Prepare an air fryer oven to preheat it at 310°F.
2. Take a loaf pan to grease it.
3. Take a bowl, add flour, cocoa powder, salt and baking soda; mix them well.
4. Take a bowl to add eggs, butter, brown sugar, oil, and vanilla mix till smooths.
5. Mix dry and wet ingredients. Fold chocolates, chips and zucchini; save a few for topping.
6. Please put this in the loaf pan and sprinkle chocolate chips on it for 30 to 35 minutes.
7. Finally, serve and enjoy it!

11. Lemon Sliced Sugar Cookies

24 min Easy 25

Nutrition Facts
Per Serving: 75 calories; protein 0.8g; carbohydrates 11.9g; fat 3g; cholesterol 12.5mg; sodium 57.4mg

Ingredients:
- ½ cup butter unsalted
- 1 pack of instant lemon pudding mix
- ½ cup sugar
- 1 egg
- 2 tbsp. milk
- 1 ½ cups all-purpose flour
- 1 tsp. baking powder
- ¼ tsp. salt
- ⅔ cup confectioners' sugar
- 2–4 tsp. lemon juice

Directions:
1. Take a bowl to add buttercream, pudding mix and sugar; mix them well for 5 to 7 minutes, then beat in milk and egg.
2. Take another bowl, add flour, baking powder, and salt; mix them well.
3. Then divide the dough into 2 halves, roll it using a rolling pin in 6-inch thick then place it in the refrigerator.
4. Prepare an air fryer oven to preheat it at 325°F. Place the ½ inch cut slices of dough in the air fryer cook for 8 to 12 minutes.
5. Take a bowl, add sugar and lemon juice, mix them and drizzle on cooked cookies; finally, serve and enjoy it!

12. Peppermint Lava Cake

30 min Medium 4

Nutrition Facts
Per Serving: 561 calories; protein 12g; carbohydrates 33.5g; fat 50.1g; cholesterol 181.8mg; sodium 249.8mg

Ingredients:
- ⅔ cup chocolate chips
- 1 cup confectioners' sugar
- ½ cup butter
- 2 eggs
- 2 egg yolks
- 1 tsp. peppermint extract
- 6 tbsp. all-purpose flour
- 2 tbsp. peppermint candies

Directions:
1. Prepare an air fryer oven to preheat it at 375°F.
2. Take a bowl, add chocolate chips, and melt it. Then add sugar, egg yolks and extracts mix them well.
3. Take a dish, grease it with butter and flour, pour the mixture in it; cook for 10 to 12 minutes at 160°F.
4. Finally, serve and enjoy it!

Holiday Special Recipes

1. Tender Juicy Smoked BBQ Ribs

65 min   Difficult   4

Nutrition Facts
Per Serving: 786 calories; protein 41.2g; carbohydrates 12.2g; fat 61.6g; cholesterol 192.1mg; sodium 5736.3mg.

Ingredients:
- 1 tbsp. liquid smoke
- 1 pack ribs
- 2 ½ tbsp. pork rub
- Pepper and salt
- ½ cup BBQ sauce

Directions:
1. Take ribs to remove its membrane cut them into half (so it easily fits in the air fryer).
2. Pour the smoked liquid on both sides of the ribs, then sprinkle pepper, pork rub and salt, mix them, cover and let them sit for 30 minutes.
3. Place these ribs in the air fryer oven, cook them at 360°F for 15 minutes.
4. After 15 minutes, turn the sides of the ribs and again cook for 15 more minutes.
5. Finally, place them on a plate, pour BBQ sauce, serve and enjoy it!

2. Beef Meatballs

35 min   Medium   4

Nutrition Facts
Per Serving: 353 calories; protein 23.8g; carbohydrates 16.5g; fat 20.5g; cholesterol 76.5mg; sodium 1456.8mg

Ingredients:
- 16 oz. lean beef (grounded)
- 4 oz. pork (grounded)
- 1 tsp. Italian seasoning
- ½ tsp. salt
- 2 cloves garlic (chopped)
- 1 egg
- ½ cup Parmesan cheese (grated)
- ⅓ cup bread crumbs and Italian seasoning

Directions:
1. Prepare an air fryer oven to preheat it at 350°F.
2. Take a bowl, add pork, beef, salt, Italian seasoning, garlic, Parmesan cheese, egg, and bread crumbs mix them well.
3. Make 16 meatballs from it. Place it in the air fryer cook for 8 minutes. After that, shake them and shake them, then cook for 2 more minutes.
4. Then transfer it in plate serve and enjoy it!

3. Kale and Bacon Stuffed Turkey Breast

60 min | Medium | 4

Nutrition Facts
Per Serving: 359 calories; protein 22.2g; carbohydrates 27g; fat 17.4g; cholesterol 32.4mg; sodium 847.5mg.

Ingredients:
- 2 lb. turkey breasts (deboned)
- Salt and pepper to taste

For preparing the filling
- 4 slices of bacon (bite-size pieces)
- 4 oz. mushrooms (sliced)
- ½ onion (diced)
- 2 cloves garlic (chopped)
- 2 cups chopped fresh kale
- ½ tsp. thyme (dried)
- ¼ tsp. sage (dried)
- ¼ tsp. salt
- ¼ tsp. black pepper
- ¼ cup parmesan cheese (shredded)

Directions:
1. Take frying pam to add slices of bacon till it becomes crispy, then add onions, mushrooms and garlic in it; cook it till mushrooms release moisture and shrinks.
2. Then add spinach to it till it becomes soft; after that, add pepper, salt, and herbs and mix it well; remove the frying pan from heat and cheese, stir it, and set aside.
3. Take a turkey breast and place a plastic wrap around it, pound thinner until it becomes ½ inch thick.
4. Then place this turkey breast on the side, down coat filling on it, fold it and tie.
5. Sprinkle salt and pepper on it. Place it in the air fryer oven, cook it for 20 minutes at 360°F. Change the side and again cook for 10 to 20 minutes.
6. Finally, place it in a tray, slice it and enjoy it!

4. Tuna Patties

25 min | Easy | 10

Nutrition Facts
Per Serving: 315 calories; protein 30.3g; carbohydrates 12.9g; fat 14.5g; cholesterol 123.6mg; sodium 407.7mg

Ingredients:
- 15 oz. canned albacore tuna (drained)
- 3 eggs
- 1 medium lemon zest
- 1 tbsp. lemon juice
- ½ cup bread crumbs
- 3 tbsp. parmesan cheese (grated)
- 1 stalk of celery (chopped)
- 3 tbsp. onion (chopped)
- ½ tsp. garlic powder
- ½ tsp. dried herbs
- ¼ tsp. Kosher salt
- Black pepper

Directions:
1. Take a bowl, add lemon zest, eggs, bread crumbs, lemon juice, onion, parmesan cheese, garlic powder, celery, dried herbs, salt and pepper mix them well.
2. A bucket of air fryer place perforated baking paper in the air fryer bucket base sprays it with cooking spray.
3. Take the mixture scoop ¼ scoop mixture and make 3 inches wide patties from it. Place them in the refrigerator for 1 hour.
4. Place them in a pan of air fryer oven, spray with cooking spray; cook them for 10 minutes at 360°F temperature flip the side halfway through.
5. Finally, serve with some sauce and enjoy it!

5. Lamb Loin Chops with Chimichurri Sauce

20 min   Easy   3

Nutrition Facts
Per Serving: 574 calories; protein 42.4g; carbohydrates 0.8g; fat 43.7g; cholesterol 168.2mg; sodium 168.5mg

Ingredients:

For preparing Lamb chops
- 1 lb. lamb chops (1-inch-thick slices)
- ½ tsp. smoked paprika
- Pepper and salt to taste
- Cooking spray

For preparing Chimichurri sauce
- ¼ cup olive oil
- ⅓ cup parsley (chopped)
- 1-2 cloves garlic (chopped)
- ¼ tsp. salt
- ¼ tsp. black pepper
- 1 to 2 pinches red pepper flakes
- 1 tbsp. lemon juice

Directions:
1. Take a bowl, add garlic, olive oil, black pepper, parsley, salt, lemon juice, and red pepper flakes, mix them well and set aside.
2. Take lamb chops to spray with cooking spray season with salt, pepper and smoked paprika, and mix them.
3. Take a bucket of air fryer, coat it with cooking spray, place lamb chops in it in a single layer cook them for 8 minutes at 380°F temperature. Change the side of chops and again cook for 4 to 8 minutes.
4. Finally, serve with chimichurri sauce and enjoy it!

6. Pork Tenderloin with Veggies

60 min   Medium   4

Nutrition Facts
Per Serving: 196 calories; protein 23.4g; carbohydrates 15.6g; fat 3.4g; cholesterol 65.4mg; sodium 904.2mg.

Ingredients:
For preparing Tenderloin
- 1 lb. Pork tenderloin
- 2 tbsp. vegetable oil
- 1 tbsp. Worcestershire sauce
- ½ tsp. garlic powder
- 2 tsp. herbs (dried)
- 1 tsp. salt
- ½ tsp. black pepper
- ½ lb. potatoes (bite-sized pieces)
- 1 carrot (1-inch cubes)

For preparing Gravy
- ½ onion (diced)
- 2 tbsp. butter
- 3 tbsp. flour
- 2 cups broth cold
- 2 tsp. Worcestershire sauce
- Salt and pepper to taste

Directions:
1. Take a large bowl; add Worcestershire sauce, oil, dried herbs, garlic powder, salt and pepper, mix them well, add potatoes, tenderloin and carrots, mix them and marinate them.
2. Take a pan of the air fryer oven, place veggies in it, and cook for 30 to 35 minutes at 370°F temperature flip if halfway through.
3. Take a frying pan, add butter, heat, add onions, and cook for 5 minutes or till onions become golden brown.
4. Take a bowl, add broth and flour and mix them. Then add salt, pepper and Worcestershire sauce to it. Decrease the temperature; cook it till it becomes thick or for 5 minutes. Place the cooked pork and veggies in a tray, serve them with warm gravy, and enjoy it!

7. Pull Apart Garlic Bread

20 min   Easy   8

Nutrition Facts
Per Serving: 265 calories; protein 4.3g; carbohydrates 25.1g; fat 16.6g; cholesterol 24mg; sodium 624.8mg

Ingredients:
- 2 tbsp. olive oil
- 2 tbsp. butter (unsalted)
- 1 tbsp. parsley (chopped)
- 1 tsp. Italian seasoning
- 4 cloves garlic (chopped)
- Salt and pepper
- 1 loaf of Sourdough bread
- 1 cup Mozzarella cheese (shredded)

Directions:
1. Take a bowl, add butter in it microwave it for 20 to 30 seconds.
2. Add garlic, parsley, olive oil, salt and pepper, and Italian seasoning in melted butter and mix them well.
3. Take bread and cut its small diamond-type shape using a serrated bread knife.
4. Add butter mix in these cuts also spread on whole bread using a cooking brush.
5. Then add shredded cheese to bread cuts.
6. Take a tray of air fryer oven and place this bread loaf in it; cook for 5 minutes at 350-Fahrenheit or till cheese melts.
7. Finally, serve and enjoy it!

8. Mushroom and Steak Bites

60 min   Medium   8

Nutrition Facts
Per Serving: 313 calories; protein 26.5g; carbohydrates 17.1g; fat 15.8g; cholesterol 115.3mg; sodium 1127.9mg

Ingredients:
- 1 lb. Steaks
- 2 tbsp. butter (melted)
- 8 oz. Mushrooms
- ½ tsp. Garlic powder
- 1 tsp. Worcestershire sauce
- Salt to taste
- Parsley (chopped)
- Chili flakes

Directions:
1. Take a bowl, add mushrooms and steak cubes in it, add melted butter, garlic powder, Worcestershire sauce, pepper and salt and mix them well.
2. Prepare air fryer oven to preheat it a 400°F for 4 minutes.
3. Take a tray of air fryer oven spread mushrooms and steak cubs in it. Cook them for 10 to 18 minutes shake them while cooking.
4. After that, take a serving tray, add these cooked mushrooms and steak, and garnish with parsley, chili flakes and butter; finally, serve and enjoy it!

Gluten-Free Recipes

1. Bacon and Egg Cups

20 min   Easy   6

Nutrition Facts
Per Serving: 174 calories; protein 26.5g; carbohydrates 0.1g; fat 12.8g; cholesterol 115.3mg; sodium 1107.9mg

Ingredients:
- 3 slices of bacon
- 6 eggs
- Salt and pepper
- 1 bunch of green onion

Directions:
1. Make the slices kinds of bacon.
2. Please put them in the bucket of air fryer and put eggs on them.
3. Sprinkle some salt and pepper.
4. Cook to 400° F for 8-10 minutes.
5. Make the rings of onion to serve with.
6. Enjoy.

2. Tonkatsu

25 min   Easy   4

Nutrition Facts
Per Serving: 573 calories; protein 41.5g; carbohydrates 17.1g; fat 25.8g; cholesterol 113.3mg; sodium 1.5g

Ingredients:
Tonkatsu
- 1 lb. pork chops
- Salt and pepper
- 3 tbsp. coconut flour
- 1 whisked egg
- 1 cup pork panko

Sauce
- ¼ cup ketchup (sugar-free)
- 2 tbsp. coconut aminos
- 2-3 tbsp. vinegar
- 1 tsp. molasses
- 1 tsp. coconut sugar
- 1 tsp. mustard
- ¼ tsp. onion powder
- ⅛ tsp. garlic powder
- ½ tsp. ginger
- ½ tsp. salt and pepper

Directions:
1. To make the sauce take a bowl and blend all the ingredients.
2. Now, season the meat with salt and pepper.
3. 3 separate bowls for coconut flour, egg and meat.
4. Put meat first in the flour, then in the egg, and put in the air fryer oven at 350°F.
5. Cook for 4-5 minutes.
6. Serve with the sauce.
7. Enjoy!
8. Serve and enjoy it!

3. Garlic Keto Croutons

10 min   Easy   10

Nutrition Facts
Per Serving: 88 calories; protein 0.8g; carbohydrates 4.1g; fat 7.7g; cholesterol 2034mg; sodium 100.7mg

Ingredients:
- 4 slices of keto bread
- 2 tbsp. butter
- ½ tsp. pepper
- 1 tsp. salt
- ½ tsp. paprika
- ½ tsp. garlic powder
- ½ tsp. parsley (dried)

Directions:
1. Cut the bread into squares.
2. Melt the butter and add spice to it.
3. Drizzle the butter seasoned with spices on the bread pieces.
4. Put in the air fryer oven at 250°F and cook for 7-8 minute
5. Let it cool.
6. Serve and enjoy!

4. Mustard Fish Sticks

20 min   Easy   4

Nutrition Facts
Per Serving: 273 calories; protein 21.5g; carbohydrates 17.1g; fat 25.8g; cholesterol 83.3mg; sodium 683mg

Ingredients:
- 1 lb. cod/white fish
- ¼ cup mayonnaise
- 2 tbsp. mustard
- 3-4 tbsp. water
- 1 cup rind panko
- ¾ tsp. cajun seasoning
- Salt and pepper to taste

Directions:
1. Spray the air fryer with cooking spray.
2. Take a bowl and mix the ingredients in it.
3. Dip the fish pieces' mayonnaise mixture and put in the air fryer oven at 200°F.
4. Cook for 5-8 minutes.
5. Serve and enjoy.

5. Chicken and Potatoes

30 min   Medium   4

Nutrition Facts
Per Serving: 393 calories; protein 48.5g; carbohydrates 17.1g; fat 25.8g; cholesterol 143.3mg; sodium 144mg

Ingredients:
- 2 lb. chicken thighs
- 1 lb. potatoes (halftone)
- 1 orange bell pepper (chopped)
- 1 red bell pepper (chopped)
- 1 tsp. garlic powder
- 1 tsp. paprika
- 1 tsp. onion powder
- ¼ tsp. cumin
- Salt and pepper to taste

Directions:
1. Mix in ingredients in a bowl.
2. Apply some oil to the chicken and then sprinkle the spice mixture over it.
3. Take potatoes and toss with oil
4. Put the chicken and potatoes in the air fryer and cook to 375° F for 10-16 minutes.
5. Serve and enjoy.

6. Apple Wedges

25 min   Easy   1

Nutrition Facts
Per Serving: 283 calories; protein 48.5g; carbohydrates 41.1g; fat 15.8g; cholesterol 143.3mg; sodium 114mg

Ingredients:
- 1 gala apple
- Salt and pepper to taste
- ¼ tsp. cinnamon

Directions:
1. Cut the apple into thin slices and sprinkle with salt and cinnamon.
2. Spray the air fryer oven with cooking spray.
3. Put the slices of apple in a single layer.
4. Cook to 375° F for 8-10 minutes.
5. Enjoy!

7. Chocolate Peanut Butter

10 min   Easy   3

Nutrition Facts
Per Serving: 323 calories; protein 48.5g; carbohydrates 47.1g; fat 10.8g; cholesterol 8.3mg; sodium 544mg

Ingredients:
- 3 oz. roasted honey peanuts
- 1 tbsp. vanilla extract
- 2 cups chocolate chips
- pinch of salt (optional)

Directions:
1. Roast the peanuts in an air fryer to 375°F for 3 minutes.
2. Take the roasted peanuts in the food processor and pulse until a full creamy texture is obtained.
3. Make sure that peanut butter is as smooth as required.
4. Add the remaining ingredients and process for 3-4 minutes till all the ingredients make a homogeneous mixture.
5. Store it in a glass container.
6. Enjoy!

8. Buffalo Wings

40 min   Medium   2-4

Nutrition Facts
Per Serving: 471 calories; protein 21.7g; carbohydrates 7.4g; fat 40.5g; cholesterol 120.3mg; sodium 1318.4mg

Ingredients:
- Cooking spray
- 2 lb. wings
- Salt
- 4 tbsp. butter
- ½ cup hot sauce
- Cheese dressing

Directions:
1. Take the air fryer oven at 200°F and spray the tray with cooking spray.
2. Sprinkle the salt of the err wings.
3. Put in the air fryer and cook for 10-12 minutes or till they are crispy brown.
4. Melt the butter in the oven and mix with the sauce.
5. Toss wings in butter sauce and serve.
6. Enjoy!

9. Garlic Parmesan Chicken Wings

25 min | Easy | 6

Nutrition Facts
Per Serving: 275 calories; protein 19.7g; carbohydrates 5.3g; fat 19.2g; cholesterol 56.4mg; sodium 245.1mg.

Ingredients:
- 2 lb. wings
- ¾ cup parmesan cheese
- 2-3 tsp. minced garlic
- 2 tsp. chopped parsley
- 1 tsp. salt and pepper

Directions:
1. Mix all the ingredients in a bowl.
2. Take wings and toss well with the mixture.
3. Place the chicken in the air fryer oven at 300°F and cook for 12-15 minutes.
4. Take the wings out of the air fryer and sprinkle some parsley and cheese.
5. Serve and enjoy!

10. Wrapped Jalapeno Poppers

30 min | Medium | 4

Nutrition Facts
Per Serving: 212 calories; protein 12g; carbohydrates 2.4g; fat 17.6g; cholesterol 51.2mg; sodium 539.4mg.

Ingredients:
- 7 jalapeno
- 6 oz. cheese
- ¾ cup shredded cheese
- ¼ tsp. black pepper
- 14 bacon strips
- ½ tsp. salt

Directions:
1. Make the slices of jalapeno.
2. Take a bowl and mix all the ingredients.
3. Fill the jalapeno with cheese mixture
4. Wrap the jalapeno in a bacon strip one by one.
5. Put it in the air fryer oven and cook to 275° F for 10-12 minutes.
6. Serve and enjoy!

Wraps and Sandwiches Recipes

1. Bacon Cheddar Grilled Cheese Sandwich

15 min   Easy   1

Nutrition Facts
Per Serving: 375 calories; protein 15.5g; carbohydrates 31g; fat 20.8g; cholesterol 58.9mg; sodium 401.3mg

Ingredients:
- 2 tsp. mayonnaise
- ½ apple
- 4 slices of cheddar cheese
- 2 slices bread
- 2 slices bacon
- 1 tsp. butter

Directions:
1. An air fryer oven is preheated up to 350°F.
2. Roll out mayo on each bread slice.
3. After that, place sliced cheese with 2 bacon pieces along with apple pieces. Finishing is done by using another cheese slice.
4. Start buttering on each side of bread and then put it in the basket of air fryers for about 180 seconds and then turn over for 180 seconds again. Let's enjoy it.

2. Tomato, Pesto and Fresh Mozzarella Grilled Cheese

15 min   Easy   4

Nutrition Facts
Per Serving: 431 calories; protein 16.3g; carbohydrates 24g; fat 29.7g; cholesterol 77.1mg; sodium 841.7mg

Ingredients:
- Sliced Tomatoes
- Sliced Mozzarella
- 2 Slices Bread
- Butter to taste
- Pesto to taste

Directions:
1. Adjust 350°F temperature to heat the air fryer oven.
2. Start one-sided buttering on each bread slice, then apply pesto on the bread top surface.
3. Topped it with tomatoes and fresh mozzarella cheese and put another bread slice with butter on its top surface.
4. For about 6 to 8 minutes, place the sandwich in the air fryer until cheese melts completely.

3. Funfetti Grilled Cheese Sandwich

15 min   Easy   2

Nutrition Facts
Per Serving: 542 calories; protein 17.8g; carbohydrates 27.7g; fat 40.5g; cholesterol 97mg; sodium 744.6mg

Ingredients:
- 2 slices of cheddar muenster
- 2 slices provolone
- 4 slices white bread
- 3 tbsp. butter

Directions:
1. Start buttering on 2 bread slices and put them on a cooking tray of the air fryer.
2. Topped with muenster cheddar, and provolone and apply butter on 2 bread slices. Place pan in cooking chamber for 10 minutes, by adjusting the temperature up to 375°F.
3. When cheese is melted and the sandwich turns brown, remove it carefully and serve warmly.

4. Crispy Fried Chicken and Waffle Grilled Chicken Sandwich

45 min   Medium   5

Nutrition Facts
Per Serving: 672 calories; protein 36.4g; carbohydrates 40g; fat 39.8g; cholesterol 99.3mg; sodium 981.4mg

Ingredients:
- 1 pinch salt
- 1 chicken breast
- ⅓ cup butter
- 1½ cups milk
- ¼ tsp. garlic
- 4 tsp. baking powder
- Cooking spray
- ⅓ cup Cheddar cheese
- 2 eggs
- ¼ tsp. Italian seasoning
- 1 tsp. salt
- 2 cups flour

Directions:
1. In a dish, add salt, garlic, seasoning flour, and baking powder and mix well.
2. Then add milk to the dish and blend it well.
3. Now Beat melted butter with milk, eggs, other dish and fold into chador cheese.
4. After preheating the air fryer oven at 250°F, cook chicken pieces for 7 minutes.
5. Now add waffle iron with cooking spray and cook till golden color by adding butter. Once all waffles are baked, assemble them and serve them.

5. Garlic Bread Grilled Cheese Sandwich

15 min | Easy | 1

Nutrition Facts
Per Serving: 624 calories; protein 26.7g; carbohydrates 28.1g; fat 45.2g; cholesterol 122.1mg; sodium 1052.2mg

Ingredients:
- 2 lb. wings
- Garlic Seasoning to taste
- 2 slices cheese
- 2 slices bread
- Butter to taste

Directions:
1. Take 2 bread slices and start buttering.
2. Put 2 slices of cheese in bread and topped it with Pat French Seasoning. Adjust air fryer temperature up to 350°F and let it for about 5 minutes, then rotate it to another side again for more than 5 minutes.

6. Air Fryer Avocado Grilled Cheese Sandwich

15 min | Easy | 4

Nutrition Facts
Per Serving: 594 calories; protein 13.7g; carbohydrates 45g; fat 45.5g; cholesterol 13.2mg; sodium 407.2mg

Ingredients:
- 4-8 slices of cheese
- 4 tbsp. butter
- 2 avocados
- 2 red peppers
- 8 slices bread

Directions:
1. Mix mashed avocado in roasted and chopped red pepper.
2. Use 4 slices of one-sided buttered bread in an air fryer basket. Put cheese slice on the bread and spread out avocado mixture then topped with cheese.
3. Adjust air fryer temperature up to 400°F. Then turn it over and fry for more than 3 minutes.

15-minutes Air Fryer Recipes

1. French Toast Stick

15 min   Easy   12

Nutrition Facts
Per Serving: 49 calories; protein 1.8g; carbohydrates 5g; fat 2.1g; cholesterol 33.1mg; sodium 77.1mg

Ingredients:
- 12 slices of toast
- 5 large-sized eggs
- 4 tbsp. melted butter
- 1 cup milk
- 1 tsp. vanilla extract
- 1 tbsp. cinnamon
- ¼ cup sugar
- Maple syrup

Directions:
1. Take the bread and make slices of it.
2. Take a large bowl and mix the milk, butter, eggs and vanilla.
3. Add sugar and cinnamon to a separate bowl.
4. Dip the breadstick in the egg mixture quickly, and then sprinkle the mixture of sugar over it.
5. Place the dipped breadsticks in the air fryer oven and cook for 8 minutes at 350°F.
6. Allow the sticks to cool.
7. Serve and enjoy!

2. Cheesy Corn Baked

10 min   Easy   12

Nutrition Facts
Per Serving: 185 calories; protein 5.7g; carbohydrates 20g; fat 9.6g; cholesterol 34.1mg; sodium 476.2mg.

Ingredients:
- 1 cup corn
- ½ cup shredded cheese
- ¼ cup breadcrumbs
- 1 tbsp. flour
- 1 beaten egg
- 1 tbsp. mayonnaise, Yogurt, Sour cream
- 1 tbsp. salt and pepper
- ½ tsp. garlic powder
- ½ tsp. onion powder

Directions:
1. Mix the ingredients in a bowl.
2. Make small balls and flatten them with the help of a palm.
3. Place in the air fryer and cook to 350° F for 4-5 minutes.
4. Serve and enjoy!

3. Crispy Broccoli

15 min   Easy   4

Nutrition Facts
Per Serving: 455 calories; protein 17.8g; carbohydrates 68.7g; fat 11.6g; cholesterol 20.3mg; sodium 1039.4mg

Ingredients:
- 4 cups fresh broccoli
- 1 tbsp. olive oil
- ⅛ tsp. salt and pepper
- ⅛ tsp. garlic powder

Directions:
1. Mix all the ingredients in a bowl and toss to coat well.
2. Place the coated broccoli in the air fryer and spray with the cooking spray.
3. Cook to 375° F for 8-10 minutes.
4. Serve and enjoy.

4. Grilled Ham and Cheese

10 min   Easy   4

Nutrition Facts
Per Serving: 740 calories; protein 39.1g; carbohydrates 30.3g; fat 51.3g; cholesterol 161.1mg; sodium 1249.8mg.

Ingredients:
- 8 bread slices
- 8 cheese slices
- 8 ham slices
- 4 tbsp. butter

Directions:
1. Apply the butter over the bread slices.
2. Put the cheese slices over it.
3. Now place ham slices on the top.
4. Add garlic powder if desired.
5. Now place the second slice of bread over it and cook to 370° F for 8-10 minutes in the air fryer.
6. Serve and enjoy!

5. Canadian Bacon and Cheese English Muffins

15 min   Easy   1

Nutrition Facts
Per Serving: 659 calories; protein 34.4g; carbohydrates 54.2g; fat 34.5g; cholesterol 85.2mg; sodium 1323.8mg.

Ingredients:

- 1 English muffin (halved)
- 2 Sliced Canadian bacon (heated)
- 1 Scrambled egg
- 1 Sliced cheese
- 1 tbsp. butter

Directions:
1. Apply butter to the muffin and toast it.
2. Place bacon, cheese and egg over it.
3. Take the air fryer and place the toast in it.
4. Just cook to 300° F for 1-2 minutes to melt the cheese.
5. Serve and enjoy!

6. Hard-boiled Eggs

15 min   Easy   6

Nutrition Facts
Per Serving: 73 calories; protein 6.4g; carbohydrates 0.4g; fat 5g; cholesterol 186 mg; sodium 71 mg.

Ingredients:

- 6 eggs

Directions:
1. Take the eggs and place them in the air fryer.
2. Cook them for 16 minutes at 200°F.
3. Take them out of the air fryer and place them in cold water.
4. Peel the eggs.
5. Serve and enjoy!

7. Crispy Delicious Bacon

11 min   Easy   6

Nutrition Facts
Per Serving: 109 calories; protein 6.4g; carbohydrates 0.3g; fat 7.6g; cholesterol 20.1mg; sodium 415mg

Ingredients:
- 11 slices of bacon

Directions:
1. Place the bacon in the air fryer oven tray.
2. Cook them for 10 minutes at 400°F.
3. For crispy texture, cook them for extra 5 minutes.
4. Take them out of the air fryer.
5. Serve and enjoy.

8. Sausage Patties

15 min   Easy   4

Nutrition Facts
Per Serving: 146 calories; protein 14.3g; carbohydrates 0.6g; fat 9g; cholesterol 45.5mg; sodium 392.3mg

Ingredients:
- 12 oz. sausage patties
- Cooking spray

Directions:
1. Place the sausages in the air fryer oven at 250°F and cook for 5-6 minutes.
2. Take them out of the air fryer.
3. Serve and enjoy!

9. Jelly Doughnuts

15 min   Easy   2

Nutrition Facts
Per Serving: 138 calories; protein 0.9g; carbohydrates 13.8g; fat 9.1g; cholesterol 8.3mg; sodium 122mg.

Ingredients:
- 1 package of home style Pillsbury Grands
- ½ cup raspberry jelly
- 1 tbsp. melted butter
- ½ cup sugar

Directions:
1. Put the rolls in the air fryer oven at 200°F and cook for 5-8 minutes.
2. Take them out of the fryer and keep them aside.
3. Take sugar in a bowl.
4. Apply butter on the doughnuts and roll them in sugar.
5. Put 2 tbsp. jelly into each doughnut with a cake tip.
6. Serve and enjoy!

10. Scrambles Eggs

12 min   Easy   2

Nutrition Facts
Per Serving: 293 calories; protein 20.4g; carbohydrates 1.2g; fat 22g; cholesterol 411.8mg; sodium 515.4mg

Ingredients:
- ⅓ tbsp. unsalted butter
- 2 tbsp. milk
- 2 eggs
- Salt and pepper
- ⅛ cup cheddar cheese

Directions:
1. Apply butter in the pan of the air fryer.
2. Whisk the milk, eggs, salt and pepper together in a bowl.
3. Place the egg mixture in the pan and cook for 2-3 minutes.
4. Then add cheese and stir.
5. Cook to 300°F or more than 2–3 minutes.
6. Remove the pan from the air fryer.
7. Serve and enjoy!

Conclusion

I love cooking since the day I got an air fryer for Christmas: it's the kitchen tool now stealing the hearts of home cooks.
And I love my collection of easy recipes for the air fryer for fish, chicken, pork, vegetable, dessert and more.

If you are trying to cut back on the amount of oil you consume, an air fryer is a great option!
If you're like me, I love to start my meals with an appetizer.
I love that I'm able to throw these appetizers in the Air Fryer and forget about them while I work around the kitchen.

They're the perfect way to start your meal.

Also, my family loves snacks and sandwiches: let's face it, the air fryer could be nick named "the snack and wraps machine".

Convenience, ease and speed!
So, without further ado...
Let's go!

Your honest review of this book is very must appreciated.
Your feedback is important to me, and it will help other Readers decide whether to read the book.
Thank you!
Cris and Karen

Want more **FREE** air fryer recipes? Send an e-mail to
topqualitycookbooks@gmail.com
to receive a Pdf with many more succulent recipes.
Enjoy

Air Fryer Cooking Chart

COOKING CONVERSION CHART

WEIGHT

IMPERIAL	METRIC
1/2 oz	15 g
1 oz	29 g
2 oz	57 g
3 oz	85 g
4 oz	113 g
5 oz	141 g
6 oz	170 g
8 oz	227 g
10 oz	283 g
12 oz	340 g
13 oz	369 g
14 oz	397 g
15 oz	425 g
1 lb	453 g

TEMPERATURE

FAHRENHEIT	CELSIUS
100 °F	37 °C
150 °F	65 °C
200 °F	93 °C
250 °F	121 °C
300 °F	150 °C
325 °F	160 °C
350 °F	180 °C
375 °F	190 °C
400 °F	200 °C
425 °F	220 °C
450 °F	230 °C
500 °F	260 °C
525 °F	274 °C
550 °F	288 °C

MEASUREMENT

CUP	ONCES	MILLILITERS	TBSP
8 cup	64 oz	1895 ml	128
6 cup	48 oz	1420 ml	96
5 cup	40 oz	1180 ml	80
4 cup	32 oz	960 ml	64
2 cup	16 oz	500 ml	32
1 cup	8 oz	250 ml	16
3/4 cup	6 oz	177 ml	12
2/3 cup	5 oz	158 ml	11
1/2 cup	4 oz	118 ml	8
3/8 cup	3 oz	90 ml	6
1/3 cup	2.5 oz	79 ml	5.5
1/4 cup	2 oz	59 ml	4
1/8 cup	1 oz	30 ml	3
1/16 cup	1/2 oz	15 ml	1